SPEAK LIFE

SPEAK LIFE

— YOU'VE GOT THE POWER —

BOOK ONE

CYNTHIA A. GOLSON-STEELE

ISBN: 0692624295
ISBN 13: 9780692624296
Library of Congress Control Number: 2016906282
Cynthia A. Golson-Steele, Evans, GA

DEDICATION

I am eternally grateful to my heavenly Father, who is faithful to his word and always causes me to triumph in victory!

To my loving parents, the late Woodrow Wilson and Polly Ann Golson. Thank you for showing what it means to press forward in the midst of opposition.

I thank God for my spiritual parents, Bishop Finace Bush Jr. and Lady Denise Bush. Thank you for covering me with your prayers and teaching me about the kingdom of God. I'm especially grateful for your wealth of wisdom.

I especially appreciate the unlimited and unconditional love, support, inspiration, and motivation that I have consistently received from my sisters (Brenda Joyce Sackel, Doretha Johnson, Doris Batchelor, and Pattie Ann Brumskill), brother (Wilson Bernard Golson Bey), brothers-in-law (Anthony Johnson and Walter Brumskill), sister-in-law (Nadine Johnson Bey), nephews, nieces, great-nieces, great-nephews, godchildren, and spiritual daughter and son.

Special thanks to my awesome church family (Crown Christian Church International), my spiritual family, my coworkers (QT Cuties),

my covenant sisters, my friends and network of supporters; I love you and appreciate all of your words of encouragement. Thank you.
In loving memory of the late Dorothy Postell, who was one of the most loving, giving, and sacrificing people I have ever known. The Lord sent Dorothy into my life a few seconds after I prayed, "Lord, I can't do this without help. Please send me help." She stepped in, rolled up her sleeves, and helped me to birth the Women's Inspirational Network, then the opening and decorating of my new business, formerly Charisma Event Centre, and she was one of the special people who encouraged and inspired me to write the series of books Speak Life. She encouraged me and supported me every chance she got. I still miss you, but I'm so glad that the Lord allowed you to be such a gigantic part of my life.

TABLE OF CONTENTS

PREFACE

THERE WERE A few special people who were catalysts for me writing *Speak Life*. First and foremost in importance is my heavenly Father. I'm grateful to God for allowing His word to be planted and to take root in my life. Yes, the day I was introduced to Christ, my life was changed forever, and I have never been the same. I desire to share with others the principles that drive me every day and the truths that frees me to be me. God's promises and prophecies keep me focused and steadfast when the gates of hell are beating against me. There is a sense of joy and peace that fills my life on a daily basis because I use words to frame my day.

My mother (who has passed on) was a woman of faith, and her faith always inspired me. She was a woman of few words; however, when she spoke, her words were faith-filled words. I saw faith in action through my mother before I saw it in anyone else.

I have been blessed to have great spiritual influences in my life. My pastor and spiritual father, Bishop Finace Bush Jr., has contributed greatly as one of the reasons I was inspired to write this book. He has been impactful to my overall growth and development as a person. He has been very impactful in planting, establishing, and expanding the kingdom of God in my heart.

I would not be able to write one word had it not been for the life lessons I've gained as a result of the trials, adversities, and victories I've had to experience. There has been much value and growth opportunity in my experiences. I've grown to appreciate the journey that has been predestined for me.

I'm grateful to be able to share the prayers, confessions, decrees, and declarations that helped me to live a more-than-conqueror's life. The Bible is like medication for my life's issues. When I speak the words in the Bible, they open my heart to faith, belief, hope, and expectation. There are no boundaries or limitations in the word of God!

Job 22:28
Thou shalt also decree a thing, and it shall be established unto thee: and the light shall shine upon thy ways.

Isaiah 55:11
So shall my word be that goeth forth out of my mouth, it shall not return unto me void, but it shall accomplish that which I please, and it shall prosper in the thing whereto I sent it.

Psalms 118:17
I will not die, but live, And declare the works and recount the illustrious acts of the Lord.

Genesis 27:7
I will not let you go unless You declare a blessing on me.

GOD IS A RESPECTER OF NO MAN; HE IS A RESPECTER OF PRINCIPLE

AFTER LIVING TWENTY-PLUS years as a born-again believer, I began to feel like something was missing in my relationship and walk with God. I was a faithful and committed believer, but at this point in my life there was a hunger for more. I was a member of a Bible-teaching church, worked in my church, prayed to God, and read the Bible, but I wanted to experience more of God, and I believed there was more God wanted me to experience. The first twenty years as a believer were spent renewing my mind, being healed and delivered from my past life's issues while adjusting to my new way of living. Although I was happy with my life and my decision to serve God for the rest of my life, I had arrived at a place of hunger.

Personally, there are times in my life when I can eat out every day for weeks at a time. I enjoy taking full advantage of having my meals prepared and served by someone else. Then there are times when I get sick at the very thought of eating out. This is when I purchase food from the grocery store and prepare it at home. This is how I felt spiritually: I could appreciate all the different messages I had heard over the years, but now I needed to spend time with God and get some answers for myself. I knew something was missing, and I needed to find it. It was time to tap into my untapped potential. I wanted to exercise my undiscovered, God-given gifts and talents. I wanted to live a more purposeful life as it related to God's kingdom. Also there were some unfulfilled dreams and visions that had been interrupted by previous trials and tribulations. Before this point of my life, I was comfortable, but now I desired to come out of my comfort zone. "Comfort Street" is a beautiful street to live on, but nothing grows on "Comfort Street." The question was how I could tap into this new realm with God. I was grateful for how far I had come, but still striving for more of my great God.

The more I sought God, I began to discover areas of my life that needed to be developed. Through seeking God and praying, I realized that I had been misapplying or not applying the correct biblical principles in order to obtain the results that I desired. This was huge and life altering. During the previous years, there were certain principles that worked in my life, but those same principles didn't apply to all aspects of my life. Silly me, trying to force the hand of God out of ignorance. One principle doesn't work for everything. Principles are not one size fits all. You have to search the Bible in order to find the principles that apply to your situation.

Example: When most believers need financial increase, they pray and pray for increase. However, prayer doesn't yield financial increase. Prayer can direct you to the correct biblical principle. The Bible reads in Luke 6:38 (NLV), "Give, and it will be given to you. You will have more than enough. It can be pushed down and shaken together and it will still run over as it is given to you. The way you give to others is the way you will receive in return." This is one bible principle that yields increase.

Another challenge I faced was speaking the word of God outwardly and aloud. The challenge was I had never disciplined myself to speak life only. I had no real value for words. However, the more I spoke the word, the more I believed it. The more I believed it, the more my faith increased. Before this change, basically, I had lived my life talking about things that I wanted and needed to change in my life; now it was time to stop talking about and start speaking to every formless, void, dark, and deep area of my life. It was time to speak relevant biblical principles into my life. I had to eliminate certain conversations in order to continue to grow and develop spiritually.

The effectiveness of the *speaking life principle* resonated in me through a sermon from my pastor titled "God Said." The scripture text was taken from Genesis 1:1–31. Genesis means "new beginning." This is what God used to change my life over the course of next ten years and is still using today. The word of God helped my faith make spiritual sense. In Genesis 1:2, the condition of the earth is described; however, verse 2 references that God "saw" (not God "described") the condition of the earth. God didn't spend His time talking about how bad the condition was, but He said or spoke to the condition, told it what to become, and the earth's condition obeyed. It was at this point that I made a decision to change how I spoke. My words were causing more hurt than healing. I thought I had it all together, not realizing that my words were not in alignment with the word of God. At times it looked quite the opposite.

Growing up, we had really good families in our neighborhood. Some of the children came from good Christian families, but you would never know it by their actions. Some of them used profanity, some were bullies, and some were thieves, among many other things. Some adults in the neighborhood would say these children weren't acting the way their parents taught them. Sometimes believers are the same way; we don't act or look like we belong to God. This had to change for me, and it will have to change for you.

I say to you, it's your time to change your reality. The purpose of outlining several verses in Genesis is to show how God demonstrated His power to speak and then released the same power to His children. As I meditated, and prayed while reading Genesis 1:3–31, my life began to evolve. I've outlined the verses that spoke to me and awakened my spirit man. In Genesis 1:3, 6, 9, 11, 14, 20, 24, 26, and 29, God, the Father, said "let" in each verse. After each "let" that God had spoken, He created something new. The creation took place at the command of His word. We too have the power to create by our words.

In verses 4, 11, 18, and 21, the scripture reads, "God saw that it was good" or "God saw that it was very good." In these verses God addresses the beauty of His work by describing it as "good" or "very good." Remember in Genesis 1:1, God didn't verbally acknowledge the bad conditions of the earth. We as believers should not verbally describe or acknowledge what we see if what we see doesn't align with the word of God.

In verses 5, 8, and 10, scripture reads "He called." God was very specific with what He called things. Before I received this revelation, I would call things and people anything I was big and bad enough to call them. I called people silly, crazy, and stupid, among other things. I called myself sick, broke, lonely, and much more. I used words like "I can't" and "that's impossible." Now I'm more specific when I speak. God is a great example.

Everything that God called was made better. In verses 7, 16, 25, and 27, the scripture reads "God made," which denotes He added His personal touch. He gave it the design that He wanted. He has the power to add His personal touch on whatever He calls into existence. We have the power through our tongue to make things better.

In verse 17, the scripture reads "God set," meaning He took the time to deliberately arrange things to serve a divinely ordered purpose. In verses 22 and 28, the term "God blessed" means for His use. He approved it and consecrated it to be used for His glory and honor. Wow! I'm sure you're saying it's time for a major overhaul.

After reading Genesis chapter 1 over and over again, I gained a new perspective on how to use my tongue. I began to have a greater appreciation and purpose for my mouth, tongue, words, and my ability to speak. The change didn't happen overnight. I'm still a work in progress. I remind myself daily of who I am and whose I am. I remind myself that I am a child of God who has been created by God in His image and after His likeness. He has given me dominion over everything He has created. Our words have the power to create life or death.

My word demolition had started to take place. I had started to give my words an assignment and purpose. My assignment was to use my tongue to change the very course of my life.

This knowledge is what started my journey to write *Speak Life: You've Got the Power.* I know this book is going to bless your life in many ways. It's designed to change your life if you apply the principles.

Acts 10:34; Romans 2:11

Proverbs 18:21
Death and life are in the power of the tongue: and they that love it shall eat the fruit thereof.

Genesis 1:2
And the earth was without form, and void; and darkness was upon the face of the deep. And the Spirit of God moved upon the face of the waters.

Why Speak Life

Why would I name a book *Speak Life*? I prayed awhile before I decided on a name. I wanted a name that would reflect the purpose of the book. The words in the book are designed to inspire every reader to speak life. To speak life is a decision and choice that I've made in order to better myself and to allow God's glory to reflect in my life. *Speak Life* is more than the name of my book. It is a huge part of my life's mission and purpose.

Daily I have the opportunity to speak into the lives of people. As a professional customer service trainer, a minister of the gospel, a teacher, a life coach, and a speaker, I'm always before people. I use each platform as an opportunity to encourage, inspire, and motivate someone. Each Sunday I stand before a congregation of people and speak life through confessions, declarations, and decrees. It's important to me to have the word of life on my tongue at all times.

I love positive word choice. I teach and often talk about positive word choice in my professional life. I believe positive word choice is necessary and beneficial. However, I must be clear in my meaning and definition of "speak life". In John 6, Jesus performed miracles before thousands. He fed five thousand with five fish and two barley loaves. The people watched the miracle, and they ate the food. Later Jesus began to speak to them about the natural temporary food in comparison to the eternal food He could give them. The people began to ask, "Who is Jesus, and what is His purpose?" The people could identify more with the natural temporary miracle, which was the fish and bread. They found it a challenge to accept Jesus as the bread of life and the eternal living word. People often lose battles due to the challenge of having to believe to receive what they cannot see in the natural. Some find it easier to give up on speaking life because what they see in the natural is contrary to what they are speaking in the Spirit by faith. Jesus offered His audience something much greater than natural food, but several left Him because they could not receive the word of life. Hear me—there is a difference in speaking positive words and Spirit-inspired, life-changing words. At times they can be the same, but not in every situation. Don't be like some who followed Jesus but couldn't go all the way. When you make the decision to speak life, make sure you believe what you are speaking and can receive the words as life. Keep speaking until you see results. In John 6:63 (AMP), Jesus said, "Every word I've spoken to you is a Spirit-word, and so it is life-making." When I use the term "speak life," I'm speaking in terms of talking, declaring, praying, and confessing what the Bible says as it aligns and pertains to the situation at hand.

There is a saying "you are what you eat." You are what you say. Whatever is on the inside will come on the outside. Out of the abundance of your heart, your mouth will speak. We have to fill our hearts with the seed of the word of God, which is much more than positive words. They are spirit-filled words.

There are some who might think it is unnecessary to carefully consider what you say, when you say it, and how you say it. Some people will be like those who stopped following Jesus when He said, "His words are spirit and life." Others will apply the principle and experience the life-changing benefits.

To speak life is a lifestyle, not just a mere process.

CYNTHIA A. GOLSON-STEELE

Luke 6:45 (KJV)
A good man out of the good treasure of his heart bringeth forth that
which is good; and an evil man out of the evil treasure of his heart
bringeth forth that which is evil: for of the abundance of the heart
his mouth speaketh.

WORDS ARE SEEDS

THERE ARE SEVERAL verses in the Bible's New Testament that reference the word "seed." The word *seed* is Greek for "sperma," as in the word "sperm." The purpose of sperm is to produce. Words are able to produce, conceive, and give birth to heavenly possibilities. The word has to be planted in your heart before it can produce. The Bible often makes reference to seed when speaking about the word of God.

I'm not a farmer, nor do I have a green thumb. However, my parents had green thumbs, and my great-uncle was a farmer. At certain times of the year, I could witness them getting ready to plant seeds for flowers, fruits, vegetables, and even grass. Each of them would purchase seeds and other related items. Whatever type of seed they planted, that is the type of harvest they would expect. My parents would plant grass seeds, flower seeds, and flowers. My great uncle would plant different types of vegetables and fruits. They would plant, water, fertilize, and nurture their seeds. In most cases it would take weeks before you were able to detect a spark of life. Both my great-uncle and parents were consistent and diligent. They knew if they continued to water and nurture what they had planted, eventually they would get results. After several weeks and/or months as an observer, I would see beautiful green grass that looked like green outdoor carpet. The flower beds would start to bloom in many colors. The fruit and vegetable garden would look transformed. Instead of seeing empty furrows, I would see rows of healthy fruits and vegetables that were ready to be picked and eaten. It's beautiful and rewarding to see the seeds you've planted come into fruition.

The word is to the kingdom of God as a natural seed is to a harvest. The same way a gardener and farmer plant seeds based on the harvest they want in return, likewise we must plant word seeds. Sow the right words, and you will reap the right harvest. A farmer doesn't sow unfruitful seeds in expectation of a fruitful harvest. Neither does a farmer sow seeds and expect an immediate harvest, but he does his part with the understanding that the seed has to go through a germination process. The word of God has to go through the process of time in our lives. The word seed system works better than any man-made system. The word seed system is fair; it won't cheat you or try to manipulate you. Seedtime and harvest have been set in place, and no man can change them. We can stop seedtime and harvest from working in our individual lives by not allowing the word to take root. When a word seed is sown, it has to be nurtured by more word seed. We can dig the seed up by speaking the wrong words, which means to speak against the word that was planted. When a farmer digs a seed up, he has to plant another seed in order to get a harvest. As believers, sometimes we plant word seeds, then dig them up. Example: A person says, "I can do all things through Christ, who strengthens me." This is a word seed that has been planted. The next day the same person says, "I'm a failure. I can't do it." The person dug up the good seed that was planted by speaking against it. Some people dig up their seeds because change doesn't happen fast enough or there is no sign of the desired results, so they go on to something else.

Once we plant word seeds, we have to leave them in the good heart soil. We must keep our heart ready to receive the word seed. We must keep bad seeds out. We should remain cognizant of the truth that each time we speak, we are sowing seeds. We have to protect the good seeds by controlling what we hear and what we say. You have to make the decision to hold yourself accountable to plant only good words in your heart.

It's imperative to hear with an understanding. Without an understanding, the word will not become fertile in your heart, and the evil one will come and snatch away what was sown in your heart.

One goal every believer should set is to take the seed of God's word and put it to work in your life by trusting and not doubting.

෴

Matthew 13:19 (NIV)
When anyone hears the message about the kingdom and does not understand it, the evil one comes and snatches away what was sown in their heart. This is the seed sown along the path.

1 Corinthians 15:33
Be not deceived: evil communications corrupt good manners.

Ephesians 4:29
Let no corrupt communication proceed out of your mouth, but that which is good to the use of edifying, that it may minister grace unto the hearers.

Mark 4:26–28
26 And he said, So is the kingdom of God, as if a man should cast seed into the ground;
27 And should sleep, and rise night and day, and the seed should spring and grow up, he knoweth not how.
28 For the earth bringeth forth fruit of herself; first the blade, then the ear, after that the full corn in the ear.

Psalms 51:10
Create in me a clean heart, O God; and renew a right spirit within me.

A HUNGER FOR MORE

AFTER DISCOVERING WHAT was missing in my desire to grow and develop spiritually and to continue in the path of walking in my God-given purpose, I continued to seek God. I had to remind myself to stay focused on the things that were happening in my life that were important to God. There will always be distractions, but you can't allow them to take you off course. In this case being hungry is good—that is, being hungry for God. The Bible says in Proverbs 16:26 (MSG), "Appetite is an incentive to work; hunger makes you work all the harder." A man's (mankind's) natural appetite will drive him to work in order to feed his hunger; likewise, your spiritual appetite will drive you to work hard spiritually to feed your spirit man. Spiritual work is to seek God more and to abide in His presence more. It was the moment I said to myself, "I know God is better than anything I can imagine, and I know He wants to manifest Himself to me in a greater way." That is the moment when things started to shift in my heart, mind, and life. I actually invited God into my life in a greater way. I stopped trying to make things happen my way and in my time. I began to allow things to happen in God's timing. I continued to speak the word of God over my life. I continued to walk by faith and not by sight. I lived in a spirit of expectation every day.

I was well on my way, growing more and trusting God more. I knew it was important to live a principles-driven life. I knew to speak life by planting word seeds. As I continued on my quest, I felt refreshed and restored, and I was ready for the next move of God, at least so I thought until this happened. Who would've thought a change in the flow of my church's worship service would have such an impact on my life? Our pastor decided to integrate corporate confession as a part of worship service. Corporate confession is the act of the congregation uniting in spirit and faith to declare the word of God. Corporate confession was a great complement to our church's worship experience, and it was especially good for me spiritually.

Including corporate confession as a part of worship was great for several reasons: it caused everyone to unite with one voice, it helped to train our spirit man to speak life, and it strengthened the congregation's faith. During corporate confession, I personally could sense a shifting taking place in the atmosphere. This was a change in the right direction.

Over time, corporate confession became such an empowering part of worship. I became drawn to speaking God's word more. Things began to change within and around me. I embraced every moment. I felt my connection and relationship with God growing even more. My prayers were being answered in a broader way. Eventually

I started to write prayers and confessions for myself, the church, and others upon request. Writing prayers and confession became a ministry for me. I was blessed to be able to share in the breakthroughs of others.

One day my pastor and first lady approached me about leading the congregation into corporate confession. After praying about it, I agreed, but mostly out of obedience and with great apprehension. I was excited and nervous at the same time. I had to keep reminding myself of my prayers to God and my quest for a deeper and more intimate relationship with Him. God will always answer our prayers, especially when we want to be used by Him. Sometimes the answer doesn't come the way we would like it to come. When I first started corporate confession, I was nervous and lacked confidence, but I never gave up. At times the atmosphere was charged with faith and excitement, and other times the people looked as if they were saying blah, blah, blah.

Nevertheless, corporate confession had ignited a fire on the inside of me. The word was like "fire shut up in my bones." It was through confession that words begin to shape my life, my world, and my surroundings. I wanted my life to align with every word that I spoke. I no longer wanted to be associated with negativity. More importantly I began to study and research the Bible on the power of words. The insight would prove to be instrumental to my calling, purpose, and destiny. Declaring the word of God can be a challenge at times. Still today I can feel my flesh and spirit at war when it's time to confess. My spirit is ready and willing to say and do the right thing, but my flesh doesn't want to fall in line. To speak life has to be a choice each time we open our mouth.

John 6:63
It is the spirit that quickeneth; the flesh profiteth nothing: the words that I speak unto you, they are spirit, and they are life.

James 1:5
If any of you lack wisdom, let him ask of God, that giveth to all men liberally, and upbraideth not; and it shall be given him.

DECREES AND DECLARATIONS

As I MENTIONED previously, it is important to understand the words that are sown in your heart. Proverbs 4:7 says, "Wisdom is the principal thing; therefore get wisdom: and with all thy getting get understanding."

From my childhood to adulthood, I was accustomed to praying silently. I didn't want anyone to hear me except God. I still pray quietly at times; however, I invest a lot of time in making decrees, declarations, and confessions, which means I'm speaking aloud. When I decree, declare, and confess, I intentionally and unapologetically release words of faith in the air. There is power and authority in speaking aloud. The better you understand the effectiveness of praying and confessing, the more powerful they will become in your life.

To declare is "to make known," "to set forth," or "to announce." An announcement or a declaration is made to make others aware of something considered to be definitive. The announcement can be a warning or sharing something great, groundbreaking, impactful, or spectacular. Example: At the end of a wedding, the groom and bride are announced as Mr. and Mrs. (using the husband's last name). This announcement is to let everyone know that the wife has taken the husband's name, and she belongs to him. There is a contract that has been made between the man and the woman and has been sealed in heaven. The husband is saying "hands off" to everyone else. When a new president takes office, he/she is announced; this means our country is under new leadership. The same is true for you as a believer; you have been declared a child of God and have gained all rights to the kingdom of God. Actually your citizenship has changed; you are now a kingdom citizen. Now you have the right to declare or make known who you are. No one can take your right away from you. To declare is to simply state and act upon your rights as a kingdom citizen. It's great to know who you are and whose you are.

When you declare, you are speaking into the atmosphere to remind the prince of the air of what has been written in the word of God concerning you. I declare the promises of God in regards to my righteousness, salvation, victory, and relationship with God. Example: I declare as a believer that I am the righteousness of God in Christ Jesus. I declare Jesus has been made unto me wisdom, righteousness, sanctification and redemption.

On the other hand, to decree is to make "a statement of truth that carries the authority of a court of order." Decrees are established to keep others from violating or dismissing the truth. When a person has a will at the time of his/her death which states that his/her possessions should be distributed a certain way, it doesn't matter what anyone else says. No one can override what has been written in the will unless they try to contest the will, which is another process that has to be proven. Another example of a decree is in the case of a husband and wife getting a divorce. Whatever was decided or established in the divorce judgment will stand. If one spouse was ordered to move out of the house, that person will have to leave. If one parent received full custody of the children, then the children will live with that parent. The court decree will stand. Since a decree carries the authority of an order by law or a judgment that has been imposed, it cannot be opposed by another. In the spiritual sense, the enemy can't change what God has set in place. Decrees are based on the word of God and in accordance to the will of God.

As a believer, to decree means to speak and call forth spiritual truths that are reinforced by God. You are superimposing God's plans and purposes over the plans and purposes of the devil. Matthew 6:10, "Thy Kingdom come, Thy Will be done on earth, as it is in heaven" (KJV). As a child of God, it's your right to decree heaven to manifest on earth. Isaiah 55:11 (KJV), "So shall my word be that goeth forth out of my mouth: it shall not return unto me void, but it shall accomplish that which I please, and it shall prosper in the thing whereto I sent it."

When we decree peace according to Psalms 29:11, we superimpose the word of God over everything that tries to bring war and confusion. When we decree according to 2 Timothy 1:7, "I have power, love and a sound mind," it causes every spirit that's associated with the spirit of fear to cease from operating in our life. When we decree according to John 10:10, a life of health and abundance, the spirit of lack and poverty is destroyed. We should always decree God's blessing upon our lives. Given this spiritual knowledge (not intellectual knowledge) combined with the authority God has given to man, we have every right to boldly declare and decree the word of God over our lives. It's imperative that we spend time decreeing and declaring instead of having idle conversations. There is power in decreeing and declaring.

❦

Proverbs 4:7
Wisdom is the principal thing; therefore get wisdom: and with all thy getting get understanding.

Job 22:28
Thou shalt also decree a thing, and it shall be established unto thee: and the light shall shine upon thy ways.

Genesis 32:26 (AMP)
Then He said, "Let me go, for day is breaking." But Jacob said, "I will not let you go unless You declare a blessing on me."

Genesis 32:29 (AMP)
Then Jacob asked Him, "Please tell me your name." But He said, "Why is it that you ask my name?" And He declared a blessing [of the covenant promises] on Jacob there.

Psalms 118:17 (AMP)
I will not die, but live, And declare the works and recount the illustrious acts of the Lord.

Psalms 51:15 (AMP)
O Lord, open my lips, That my mouth may declare Your praise.

Luke 12:8 (AMP)
I say to you, whoever declares openly and confesses me
before men [speaking freely of me as his Lord], the Son
of Man also will declare openly and confess him [as one
of His own] before the angels of God.

Isaiah 55:11
So shall my word be that goeth forth out of my mouth: it
shall not return unto me void, but it shall accomplish that
which I please, and it shall prosper in the thing whereto I
sent it.

Isaiah 43:26
Put me in remembrance: let us plead together: declare
thou, that thou mayest be justified.

Psalms 81:10 (NIV)
Open wide your mouth and I will fill it.

MY ACCOUNT

THE BIBLE IS filled with men and women who were inspired by the Holy Spirit to share their personal testimonies of their response to the word and faith in action. This book, *Speak Life*, is my account of how the word of God works in my life. Of course, speaking life, praying, and confessing don't work by themselves. There are other biblical principles that work in conjunction with speaking life. However, this precious book is a great place to start!

It gives me joy to share with you some of the testimonies, analogies, prayers, and confessions of faith that have brought me through some of the most tumultuous times in my life. I pray that they bless your life as much as they have blessed mine.

I'm no different from anyone. I have to stand in the midst of opposition and adverse circumstances called trials and tribulations. I have to maintain a consistent prayer life and an ongoing relationship with God. In the most difficult times, I have to constantly remind myself of the importance of speaking to and not talking about what I'm facing. In doing so, I'm inspired to write a confession to release into the atmosphere what the Bible says about the trial. It makes me an overcomer. It builds my faith in the word of God and keeps the answer in front of me.

Several years ago, Bishop Finace Bush Jr. shared twelve foundational reasons to confess and declare the word of God. I would like to share them with you.

Twelve Foundational Reasons to Confess and Declare the Word of God

1. It is the way I sow seeds in the kingdom.
2. It causes faith to come.
3. It renews my mind to the word of God.
4. It keeps the answer before me.
5. It changes my heart.
6. It sets the laws of faith in motion my life.
7. It puts the angels to work for me.
8. It makes me (mentally) conscious of the spiritual and supernatural realm.
9. It raises my expectations to a higher degree. Words initiate the exchange of faith.
10. It voids (cancels) out my excuse for carnality (carnal exchanges).
11. It demands I think through my options.
12. It demands I walk in the spirit.

Mark 4; Mark 4:14; Romans 12:2; Joshua 1:8; Romans 10:17; Psalms 103:20; Proverbs 23:7

The Word Is Like Medicine

I WOULD LIKE to share this brief and impactful story with you. There was a child who was born into wealth. She was an only child. She had everything a child could imagine. She had loving parents, a big house that looked like a castle that sat on a hill, several pretty cars, and even maids to clean her room. She wore such nice clothes. It was as if she never wore the same outfit twice. At Christmas her home was filled with toys. She had bikes, battery-operated cars, dolls, dollhouses, board games, computers, electronics, multiple Christmas trees, and so much more. She was the most popular person in school, with many friends. She was a cheerleader and played many musical instruments. Above all else, she could sing very well. I knew this because not only did we attend the same school, but the same church too. There was one thing that always stood out about this girl. She could never do anything for an extended period of time. She was very inconsistent. She liked to start and stop. She would be excited in the beginning, as if this was it. Each month she had a new favorite thing. Her parents, teachers, and even her pastor would try to get her to focus on one thing, but they were unsuccessful.

I remember her changing her major in college several times. However, she did graduate from college. During college she would come home during breaks and would always come to church, dressed in her nice apparel and driving the latest and greatest car. She was always sweet and well mannered. After she graduated from college, she purchased a home in her hometown. She continued to attend service often. One Sunday during service, she asked the pastor if she could speak. He allowed her to speak. Her parents joined her at the front of church. She began by talking about how good God had been to her and how grateful she was to her parents for giving her such a privileged life. She then shared that she had been recently diagnosed with a rare blood disease. If the blood disorder wasn't treated, then over time it would cause damage to her major organs. Her doctor told her there was no cure, but it could be well managed with a strict and specific treatment plan. She stated that as long as she followed the treatment plan, she would be able to lead a productive life. She said the treatment plan was easy, but very specific. Her treatment included that she take one pill three times a day at the same time every day for one year. She told us about the mild side effects, the light nausea, and some tingling in her fingers and toes. She asked the congregation to pray for her.

The most important part of the treatment was to take each dosage at the same time each day to avoid a total relapse. She explained that missing dosages over time would cause her to have a relapse. Each relapse and restart would take a toll on her body, mainly her organs. After she finished sharing her story with the congregation, everyone was sad but relieved knowing the condition was easily treated. The pastor prayed for her and told her it would be fine. Also, he encouraged her to take her medication as prescribed. After service everyone encouraged her, and some even told her to set a reminder in the phone to make sure she took the medicine each day and on time. She figured there wasn't a need to be reminded of taking the medicine. After all, it was the key to keeping her alive.

She started the treatment, and the first few months were like clockwork. She was taking her medication on time every day. She experienced the side effects, but they were so mild. They didn't stop or slow her down. She was able to work at her parents' company, and she kept coming to church and kept serving. After consistently seeing her at church for a while, I noticed that I stopped seeing her. The pastor later informed the congregation that she'd had a relapse. He said she was taking her medicine, keeping her doctor's appointments, and having her blood work done. When her blood count had increased to a good level, she decided that she no longer needed to take the medicine every day. She stopped taking the medicine as prescribed.

One day she collapsed at work and had to be rushed to the hospital. Although she had gotten to the hospital in time, she hadn't been to church because she was at home recuperating. The relapse had taken a toll on her kidneys and heart. She had to restart her treatment immediately. She was obedient and excited about restarting her treatment, because she needed to get better in order to resume her lifestyle. A few weeks later she was back to church. She looked a little tired, but she kept pressing. This time when she started her treatment, she began to network with some of the ladies at church, and they kept a check to make sure she was taking her medicine as prescribed. Again she was doing great. She was back to singing with the praise team and choir. She had returned to work.

After a few months, she agreed to work out of town for her parents' company. Everything was fine for a while until she started to miss taking her meds and having her blood work done. While working out of town, she had to be admitted to the hospital again. This time her situation was worse than the last time. This time was harder on her body than before.

Over the course of twelve months, she had to be admitted to the hospital over four times. The fourth time was the worst. She received some devastating news. She was told that she had severe damage to her heart, and it would not get better. Also, her kidneys were not functioning properly, and eventually she would need dialysis. The doctors told her that they could keep her comfortable, but the treatment wouldn't have the same impact. She asked them to increase the dosage. She reassured them that she would take the medicine as prescribed and would never miss a dosage, but the doctor told her that medicine would not help at this time. She reminded herself of all the times she was told to take the medicine as prescribed. She allowed a bad habit to stop her. The habit of starting and stopping. The habit of not being consistent. Being consistent was always a challenge to her, and now it had finally caught up with her. She ended up spending her last days being bedbound at a young age.

I took that time to share this story with you as a way to help you understand the importance of consistency in speaking life. Your words are like your spiritual medicine, and your continually speaking them is like the treatment plan. The more you speak the right words, the stronger your spirit man will become. Your words are your lifeline or your death line. You have to be intentional, consistent, and diligent when you speak.

In this life, you will have many battles to fight. What if our battles in life were considered to be conditions that need treatment? What if one very important element to successfully winning was to speak life-giving words such as the ones that are loaded in the Holy Bible? What if the success of your spiritual treatment plan was contingent upon you speaking life over every situation, and each time you chose not to speak life, you voided out your healing? Each time you speak life, the angels in heaven start to work on your behalf. On the other hand, what if every time you spoke death, defeating words, the angels stopped working for you and returned to their starting point to wait for you to put them to work again? What if every time you spoke death, the devil and his workers started working on your behalf to bring every negative and death-giving word to pass in your life? Would you change your words?

Remember, the devil's goal is to damage your spiritual organs, which include faith, hope, love, peace, joy, and many others. He damages your spiritual organs by convincing you that everything that's happening to you is working against you. According to John 10:10, "The thief cometh not, but for to steal, and to kill, and to destroy; I am come that they might have life, and that they might have it more abundantly." The devil is a thief. When you believe his lies, you will speak the lies and not the truth. When you open your mouth to speak, you have to ask yourself if you are about to speak life or speak death.

It's time to put an end to the life-diminishing behavior. You are destroying your own life by giving the devil admonition through your words. Don't end up like the young lady in the story. Start your word treatment today. You will begin to frame your world by your words. You can be consistent, diligent, and disciplined with your words.

Your words have power. Let's activate the power!

Faith without Works Is Dead

THE DEVIL WILL do everything in his power to keep you from speaking life. After several years of leading corporate confession, writing confessions, counseling, coaching, and constantly talking on the phone, I was challenged by my very own words.

I had started to experience pain in my face. The pain slowly progressed. It got to the point that it was painful to open my mouth, to speak or chew. I couldn't figure out what was happening. I was in constant pain. There was no painkiller that would ease the pain. Finally, I went to see my doctor, and she ran tests. I was diagnosed with a condition called trigeminal neuralgia. This is a condition that affects the nerves in the upper, middle, and lower parts of the face. The condition is considered to be progressive and over time can cause permanent damage to the nerves in the face to the point where it's best not to open your mouth at all. In the worst-case scenario, the pain and medication could leave a person depressed to the point of becoming bedridden.

The news was very alarming and devastating. At first I wondered why this affliction had happened to me. I thought surely God wants me to declare His word, and how could I if I'm not able to speak? The doctor gave me a prescription, which had numerous side effects. I couldn't take the medicine and continue to have a "normal" life. I asked questions and did research, but there were very few options. It was at this point I had to recall the truth that "death and life are in the power of my tongue." I'm not anti-medicine, but this medicine wasn't going to really help my condition; it would only create another condition. I began to speak to my body and commanded it be healed. There were things that I stopped doing, such as chewing gum and eating hard-to-chew foods. I needed to take away all of the enemy's weapons in order to render him helpless. I declared my healing every day. I endured the pain, but I never stopped confessing my healing. My faith, beliefs, expectations, desires, and words were being challenged. Also, the faith and belief of many others were on the line. When you speak power words, the forces of darkness will come after your words to prove your words as powerless. I did what any good soldier would do. I geared up and went to war with the gear that I needed: the principles of healing faith, hope, belief, and God's word. I knew no weapon that was formed against me would prosper. I knew by Jesus's stripes I was healed. I knew greater was Jesus in me than he that was in the world. I spoke healing over my body day in and day out. The pain got worse before it got better, but as I write I can't remember the last time I've been in pain. It has been years. God healed me according to His words that I declared over my body.

Faith is confidence in what you hope for and assurance about what you do not see. Keep speaking life even when you can't see it in the natural. Eventually the spirit and heavenly realm will connect with your natural realm to give you your earthen reality.

James 2:18 (KJV)
Yea, a man may say, Thou hast faith, and I have works: shew me thy faith without thy works, and I will shew thee my faith by my works.

James 2:20 (KJV)
But wilt thou know, O vain man, that faith without works is dead?

James 2:26 (KJV)
For as the body without the spirit is dead, so faith without works is dead also.

Right Alignment

I HAVE A love for very nice cars. Some of my favorite cars are the Mercedes G-Wagon, Porsche Panamera, Porsche Cayenne, and Maybach. A hobby of mine is to test drive the finest of cars. I have driven to various states just to test drive certain cars. This is a thrill, adventure, and another form of therapy for me. On the other hand, it's a challenge for me to keep my personal cars maintained. I often miss important maintenance appointments. I have to purchase a new or new-used car approximately every three years because of unnecessary wear and tear.

Several years ago, I had a very nice car. I enjoyed driving this car, but at some point my steering wheel was no longer centered. Something wasn't right, and I didn't know why or what, but the car still moved without any problems, so I kept driving. One day a male friend of mine had to drive my car. He was shocked at how the steering wheel, tires, and the car pulled to one side. He asked me had I noticed the steering wheel or the car pulling to one side. My answer was yes, but I thought it was fine. I couldn't see any harm being done.

"Oh no," he said, "you need a wheel alignment." I had never heard of a wheel alignment.

An alignment is needed over a span of time as a part of standard automobile maintenance. An alignment consists of adjusting the angles of the wheels so that they are set at a certain specification. Having an alignment done in a timely manner reduces tire wear and keeps the vehicle traveling straight and without "pulling" to one side. It is advisable to do the alignment of a new car after the first three thousand miles even if there aren't any evident signs of needing one. With a used car, you may notice that you need an alignment because of uneven tire wear and a pull/drifting to the left or right. If you ignore the need for an alignment, it could cause tire wear that leads to frequent replacement of tires and you having to spend unnecessary money on replacing tires. Ignoring the fact that a wheel alignment is needed can cause irritation and/or fatigue while driving the car, which is not good. Overall, it is in your best interest to have your car checked in a timely manner to avoid paying unnecessary fees. The other thing is, when you read your owner's manual, it will tell you when to have your car serviced. I ignored all the warning signs.

My love for cars and my failure to recognize the need for an alignment is very similar to the state we can find ourselves in spiritually. We love God and enjoy seeing His marvelous works. We even enjoy talking about how He works. Serving God can be like looking at all of those pretty cars but neglecting your own pretty car. Our lives can get out of line when we don't service and properly maintenance them. When you see an area of your life going off course or getting out of line, you should make adjustments quickly to correct the problem.

I mean whenever a situation, trial, or test arises in your life, you have access through the power of God to speak the word of God over the situation. Have faith, believe, and make sure your words align with the Bible. It's important to speak the word even when it's contrary to what you see in the natural. Reread Genesis 1 when you need to remind yourself of how God handled the situation when He saw the condition of the earth. God didn't complain about what He saw, but He spoke the word, and He called into existence what He wanted the earth to become. Utilize your tongue to help keep your life aligned.

Proverbs 18:21 (NIV); Isaiah 55:11 (KJV); 1 Peter 3:10 (KJV)

THE ROAD MAP

I USED TO travel the East Coast a lot with my father. We would travel from New York to South Carolina to visit family. I traveled with him to help drive and to keep him company. While I traveled with him, he taught me how to read a road map. This was when people still used maps to travel because there was no such thing as Google or GPS. We had a world map, which showed the continents and location of every country in the world. I enjoyed seeing which continent each country was located in. Some countries I had never heard of. I remember him showing me the map of North America, then the map of the United States of America. Over time I became very familiar with the map of the United States of America because that was the one we used most often. Imagine how overwhelming it was trying to map out my drive from Philadelphia, Pennsylvania, to Columbia, South Carolina, by looking at the world map or the whole US map. That would have been a lot to digest all at once. I only needed the map that covered the east coast.

The Holy Bible has the answer to everything that we could ever face, but we would become overwhelmed if we attempted to search for every answer all at once. That would be like looking at the world map while trying to find one small city. It is good to study the whole Bible, and it is good to study the world map, but when it comes to traveling to a specific place, you have to narrow your search or target your search to one place.

My desire to write *Speak Life* is to point the believers in the right direction to target their words toward a specific area of need. *Speak Life* can never replace the Bible, but it can help you along the way. The Bible is our basic instructions before leaving earth, and nothing can ever take its place. In *Speak Life*, I wasn't able to write a prayer or confession for every biblical principle, but I believe I've covered the most common concerns. As I share some of the confessions that have helped me over the years, I urge you to start writing your own confessions and pass them on to others. We must raise our expectation in order to point believers to speak the promises of God over their problems.

We live in a time when the demand for words has lessened. A large part of this is due to a rise in communication through social media and technology such as Instagram, Twitter, Facebook, and texting. With technology on the rise, the opportunity to communicate effectively has declined. Our society is trying to replace words with short-form texting and pictures. There is a saying that "a picture is worth a thousand words." I've seen some beautiful pictures, and there is a lot that a picture can depict, but pictures, photographs, selfies, etc., cannot replace words. Words open our heart and soul to human thoughts, feelings, and emotions. It's out of the abundance of the heart that the mouth speaks. Think back to Genesis 1: God framed the whole world by using words. Words have the power to awaken our imagination and creative ability. Without the speaking of words, things cannot change.

I'm always encouraging people to consider what they say before they say it. Words are like actions: they have consequences. In *Speak Life*, I've written several powerful and anointed confessions and prayers. I ask that you read and declare them in a spirit of faith and expectation. Open yourself to receive the change that is about to happen in your life. You will never be the same. You will find it difficult to speak idle and meaningless words.

SPEAK LIFE

CONFESSIONS AND PRAYERS

SPEAK LIFE FOR SPIRITUAL EMPOWERMENT

THIS IS MY YEAR

I confess as a child of the most High God that (20_ _) is my year!
I decree the year of (20_ _) to be an exceptional year. Prophecies,
promises, dreams, and visions will come to pass. I decree this is going
to be a year of surprises. God is going to amaze me with His goodness.
I'm stepping into a new season. I'm letting go of what didn't work in
(20_ _). I have a new attitude, and I have enlarged my vision. I have a
new fire and greater expectancy. This year I'm pressing forward!

I have a different perspective on life. I see only the good things God
has in store for my present and my future. I'm looking through
the eyes of faith. I can see the anointing of God on my life. He has
anointed me to accomplish my dreams. I am anointed to overcome
any obstacle. I am equipped and empowered by God to live the
abundant life He has prepared for me.

This is the year things are going to change. God has released His favor
in a greater way. I have sown the seeds, I've planted, I've watered, and
I've been faithful. Now I'm about to come into my harvest. This is my
year for a breakthrough! This is my "above and beyond" year, and I
claim victory for my family, friends, church, and myself in Jesus's name!

I declare God's goodness and faithfulness in my life. I take the limits
off of my thinking and lift my eyes unto the hills from which comes
my help. My help comes from the Lord, and this is the year that the

Lord will help me to move forward. This year I will read, study, pray, confess, worship, and praise God more. I thank God in advance for the great things that will manifest in my life. I thank you, Lord, for what you are doing right now.

I will bless the Lord at all times, and His praise shall continually be in my mouth.

I will live as I was created to live. I was created to be whole, and my faith makes me whole. I'm still alive because God has greater victories in store for me. My faith, expectations, and hope are right now. God is working in my favor right now in this hour.

I declare that this year and in future years, I will allow your word to continuously set me free. I will stand strong. I will stay faithful to your word. I will dwell in the secret place of the Most High. I will rest in the shadow of the Almighty. I will say the Lord is my refuge and my fortress, my God in whom I trust.

I declare the year of (20_ _) as my year!
Glory to God!

ﾟ⌒ﾟ⌒

STEADFAST AND UNMOVABLE

I make this declaration in accordance with Hebrews 10:23 and Romans 5:3–5. I am steadfast, unmovable, and always abounding in the work of the Lord. I know my labor is not in vain. Furthermore, I declare that I glory in my tribulations, knowing that the trying of my faith works patience; and patience, experience; and experience, hope; and hope makes me not ashamed because the love of God is being shed abroad in my heart by the Holy Ghost.

I hold fast to the confession and profession of my faith. I don't waiver or stagger at the promises of God through unbelief, but I remain strong in faith and always give glory to God. I'm not moved by circumstances. I am moved by faith. My God is faithful to who promises.

Hebrews 10:23; Romans 5:3–5

ﾟ⌒ﾟ⌒

Psalm 1

I am blessed in accordance with Psalm 1. I am blessed because I do not walk in the counsel of the ungodly, nor do I stand in the way of sinners, nor do I sit in the seat of the scornful; but my delight is in the law of the Lord; and in his law, I meditate day and night.

I am like a tree planted by the rivers of water that brings forth my fruit (increase) in my season; my leaf will not wither; and whatsoever I do shall prosper.

For the Lord know my ways, and I will not perish. In Jesus's name!

STANDING RIGHT WITH GOD

I thank you, Jesus, for being made sin so that I might become the righteousness of God. I confess that I'm righteous and in right standing with God Almighty through Jesus Christ, my Savior. I stand in the will of God, and I follow in his paths. My God is leading me in the paths of righteousness for his name's sake. This right standing keeps me growing in God's grace, and it shuts the door to the enemy. Daily I stand in God's grace. I strive to live righteously and to remain in right standing with God.

Isaiah 26:7 (NIV)

SPEAK LIFE WHEN TAKING CHARGE OF YOUR REALITY

Put on Your Armor Daily

Father, I thank you for this day. I thank you for the opportunity to see another day. Father, I put on my full armor. I put on the helmet of salvation, the breastplate of righteousness, the shield of faith, the sword of the spirit, the belt of truth, and the shoes of peace, and I cover my armor with the blood of Jesus. Father, I ask you to give your angels charge over me (also call out by name your children and your spouse) as we go forth today to keep us in all of our ways. Set your hedge of protection around us to protect us.

Father, I thank you for the knowledge of your will with all wisdom and spiritual understanding. I thank you for your revelation knowledge flowing freely through me and for giving me the gift of might to bring to pass everything you have purposed for this day. Father, I thank you for allowing goodness and mercy to follow me all the days of my life and for favor going before me in every exchange I make. I thank you for a shield of favor surrounding me wherever I go.

Father, because I have given, I thank you for causing men to give unto me good measure, pressed down, shaken together, and running over today. Father, I thank you that today I live the first-class life without paying the first-class price. I thank you for calling me blessed and empowering me to prosper because I walk not after the counsel of the ungodly, nor do I stand in the way of sinners, nor do I sit in the seat of the scornful today, but I delight myself in your law, and I meditate on your law night and day. Because I do this, I am like a tree planted by the rivers of water. I bring forth fruit in my season, and my leaves do not wither. Whatever I do prospers. I am diligent in my business, and I thank you for making me to stand before kings and not mean men.

Father, I thank you for allowing me to represent your kingdom today. I will draw men to you with my Christ-like character and by showing the love of Christ. I thank you for a productive day in Jesus's name.

Ephesians 6:10–17; Psalms 1:1; Psalms 91:11; Job 1:10; Psalms 23:6; Psalms 5:12; Luke 6:38; Proverbs 22:29

Written and dedicated by Cynthia Walker

FEARLESS

I declare that I don't fret or have anxiety about anything. My complete trust is in God, and he has never failed me.

I am not moved by trials. In the midst of my trials, my faith will remain strong. Trials and tribulations can only cause me to grow. I will count it all joy when I fall into manifold temptations. I know that my faith is being tried, and the proving of my faith will bring about more patience in my life. By the grace of God, I will let patience have its perfect work that I may be made perfect and entire, lacking in nothing. In the name of Jesus!

James 1:2–11

OVERCOMING FEAR

I decree and declare I do not have fear. I know God is with me. He gives me strength, and he upholds me with his right hand (the hand of favor and pleasures forever more).

I do not fear because there is no love in fear. God's perfect love casts out and removes all fear from my life. Fear no longer torments me because God's love has been perfected in me.

I decree that when I lie down, I lie down in peace, and my sleep is sweet. I am not afraid of sudden fear or death. I will not be afraid or discouraged, for the Lord fights on my behalf. The Lord is a shield around me. He is the one who lifts my head. I will not fear though tens of thousands surround me on every side. I trust my heavenly Father above all else. Daily I am kept and sustained by the hand of God. Fear is false evidence appearing real. I do not have a spirit of fear. I have a spirit of power, love, and a sound mind. In the name of Jesus!

Isaiah 41:10; Proverbs 3:24; Psalms 3:2–6; Joshua 10:25; 1 John 4:18

FACING A DIFFICULT SITUATION

I confess that I can do all things through Christ, who strengthens me. I am equipped with everything I need to live a victorious life. No matter how difficult things may seem in the natural, I will rejoice because the sufferings of this present time are not worthy to be compared with the glory that shall be revealed in me.
By faith I receive the full armor of Jesus Christ, and I am able to stand strong and overcome every obstacle. I am empowered by God to walk through difficult situations in my life. I am an overcomer. This difficult situation is making me stronger and better. In the name of Jesus!

Ephesians 6:11; Psalms 37:23; Romans 8:18

ᢒᢒᢇ ᢇᢒᢓ

Forgiveness

I decree and declare that forgiveness is a part of my everyday life. Jesus forgives me when I trespass. I confess my sins, and Jesus, being faithful and just, forgives my sins and purifies me from all unrighteousness. I take pleasure in forgiving those who trespass against me. Forgiveness comes easier and easier for me. I renounce the hurt, pain, rejection, and negative words from my past. I forgive each and every person who has done me wrong.

I have grown beyond holding grudges. I can't control the actions of others, but I can control my actions. I choose to forgive and show love.

Ephesians 1:7; 1 John 1:9

THE CHARACTER OF GOD

I decree and declare that I strive daily to live peaceably with others.
I challenge myself to be kind and generous and to show love to others. I keep the sayings of God on my lips, and I commit to speaking
them in every conversation.

I avoid being contentious, selfish, full of strife, conceited, and arro-
gant. I realize that no one wants to communicate with a know-it-all
person. I further declare that I let no corrupt communication come
out of my mouth, but I communicate only that which is good for
building up, that which is fit for the occasion, and that which gives
grace to those who hear.

I aim for my speech to be full of grace, seasoned with salt, so that I
will know how to respond to each person. I speak the right words
at the right time. I am quick to hear and slow to speak and slow to
anger. I speak the truth in love. In the name of Jesus!

Galatians 5:22–26; Proverbs 28:12; Isaiah 54:17;
Ephesians 4:11–16, 29; Colossians 4:6; Psalms 25:11

Successful Workday

I bless and praise God for my job and my coworkers. I thank God in advance for allowing us to work in a safe and protected atmosphere. Each day I embrace and receive the blessing of the ministry, talents, gifts, and skills that God has given me through His mercy. When I'm challenged at work, by God's blessing I will not lose heart, but rather I renounce all secret and shameful ways. I will not practice advancing myself through deceptive means or distorting the word of God. I will not give up or throw in the towel when I run into hard times. I will not twist God's word to suit myself, and I will not manipulate and maneuver behind the scenes to advance myself.

I trust God and will allow His plan to play out in every circumstance and every situation. I will not conform to the world's cutthroat system. I will allow the light of God's glory to shine in my heart and Christ's glory to be upon my face, because I have God's treasure on the inside. God's treasure causes me to walk in integrity.

I further declare that when things try to press me on every side, they will never fully crush me. When things become perplexed, I will not be despaired. When I am persecuted, falsely accused, or treated unfairly, I know God will never abandon me. When I am struck down, I will not be destroyed. Daily I will carry about in my body as a reminder the death of Jesus, so the life of Jesus may also be revealed in my body each and every day. I confess this for myself and my coworkers. In the name of Jesus!

2 Corinthians 4:1–13

SPEAK LIFE OVER YOUR FAMILY

Family

Father, I thank you for my family. I'm grateful for our oneness and harmony. I cover my spouse and children under the blood of Jesus. I speak divine protection over them as they travel to and from work and school. I speak health and wellness over my family. May the love, unity, and peace that you have given us spread to other families in our church and our community. In the name of Jesus.

Marriage

We speak a blessing over our marriage. We decree and declare because we keep you first, you cause us to unite as one voice. We speak gentle and kind words to each other, even when there is conflict. We honor our marital covenant. We dedicate our bodies to you and to each other only. We will not defile our bed. We reverence and fear God. We walk in obedience to God's word. Together we take our concerns to God in prayer.

Husband

Father, I thank you for my husband. My husband is blessed with favor with God and man. I am my husband's good thing. He loves me as Christ loves the church and gave himself for it. My husband is a man of integrity. He keeps me as the apple of his eye. My husband sees me as a strong woman, but he honors me as the weaker vessel. My husband and I are one flesh. My husband is a great provider. He loves God and seeks the wisdom of God when making decisions for our family.

WIFE

Father, I thank you for my wife. I thank you that she knows who she is in Christ. She is strong, secure, and confident. She is a great mother to our children. I thank you for how my wife submits and respects me as unto the Lord. She helps to bring out the best in me. She makes our house a home. My wife is like a fruitful vine by the side of our home. My wife and I are one flesh. My wife builds our home and does not tear it down. My wife will do me good all the days of her life. We are one in Christ! In the name of Jesus!

1 Peter 3:7; Proverbs 18:22; Genesis 2:24; Proverbs 14:1

CHILDREN

I speak life over my children. My children are a gift from God. I decree and declare that my children are a heritage from the Lord. I train my children in the way they should go so that when they are old, they will not depart from my training.

I declare my children are respectful to their elders. They are obedient in the Lord and are very honorable. Therefore, I decree that my children will be blessed with long life. My children will be taught by the Lord, and great will be the peace of my children.

I declare as a parent that I do not provoke my children to anger, but I bring them up in the discipline and instruction of the Lord. My children are like olive plants round about thy table. I confess that I will enjoy the fruit of my labor with my children. They will bring me joy and not shame. In the name of Jesus!

Psalms 127:3; Proverbs 22:6; Proverbs 29:15; Isaiah 54:13

BETTER RELATIONSHIPS WITH FAMILY AND FRIENDS

I confess that I have strong relationships with my friends and my family. My friends and I make each other better, like iron sharpens iron.

My family and friends love me at all times, and I love them at all times. We love each other unconditionally. We appreciate our differences and accept each other the way God made us. We love each other through our differences. Our relationships continue to prosper and grow. My family and friends are reliable.

I am available for them when they need me, and they are available for me when I need them. We fellowship to make each better. If I fall, my family and friends are there to help pick me up, and I'm there to pick them up if they fall.

I do not choose my friends; I allow God to send the right people in my life. God allows me to meet the right people at the right time. Therefore, I declare that I have flourishing relationships. I declare that I make divine and purposeful connections. I show myself friendly, and my friendships are increasing.

I walk with the wise, and I am made wise. I allow God to work in me and through me to restore and maintain good relationships with my family and friends.

Proverbs 27:17; Proverbs 18:24; Proverbs 17:17; Proverbs 13:20

SUCCESSFUL SCHOOL DAY

I declare that I have the best attitude today as I prepare for school. I declare my attitude will continue to please God throughout today.

I desire to please God, my parents, and myself by doing my very best and being a light to others. I will be helpful and respectful to my teachers and classmates.

I will strive for excellence in every subject. I will not become discouraged when a subject is challenging and difficult. I will pray and ask God for wisdom and understanding. I will trust God to help me one day at a time.

I pray that my school will be a safe place to attend—a place that is free of crime, peer pressure, and bullying.
I pray for God-fearing teachers and students. Lord, I ask that my school be filled with love and not hate. Holy Spirit, I ask that you would remain in my school.

In the name of Jesus!

School-Day Confession

(Have children repeat after you each morning to put on armor of God.)

Father, I thank you for this day. I thank you for allowing me to wake up this morning. Father, I ask you to watch over me as I go forth today. Cover me in the blood of Jesus and set your hedge of protection around me to protect me. I ask you to encamp your angels in front of me, behind me, to the left of me, to the right of me, above me, and underneath me. Father, I put on the helmet of salvation, the breastplate of righteousness, the shield of faith, the sword of the spirit, the belt of truth, and the shoes of peace, and I cover my armor in the blood of Jesus.

Father, I thank you that I am equipped to learn today. I excel in everything I do. Everything I put my hands to do prospers. I pass every test with flying colors because I can do all things through Christ, who strengthens me. I thank you for my teachers being anointed to teach me. They have anointed ideas, concepts, and inventions that help me to learn. I learn with ease because greater is he within me than he that is in the world. I am a light to those around me that draws men to you. I display the character of Christ wherever I go.

I will have a good day because this is the day the Lord has made. I will rejoice and be glad in it in Jesus's name.

Ephesians 6:10–17; Philippians 4:13; 1 John 4:4; Psalms 118:24; Job 1:10

Written and dedicated by Cynthia Walker

~~~~~

LIVING SINGLE

I confess that my mind is free from anxieties and impure thoughts. Right now I'm focused on the things of God and how I may please the Lord. I am united in spirit with the Lord.

I treat my body as the temple of the Holy Spirit and as a gift from God. My body does not belong to me, but to God. I have been bought with a price and have been made God's own. I honor and bring God glory with my spirit, soul, and body.

I believe that as I delight myself in the Lord, He will give me the desires of my heart. I desire to be married in the future. I believe that I'm being prepared to be a loving spouse for my mate. I will patiently wait on the Lord and will be of good courage. I will remain in expectation and will not lose heart. I will continue to develop myself physically and spiritually. As I wait on God, He is preparing my future spouse. When we meet, we both shall be two whole people who will become one.

Hallelujah!

1 Corinthians 7:32–35; Psalms 128:3; Ephesians 3:16;
Psalms 89:34; Deuteronomy 28:1–14

~~~~~

My Family, Friends, Church, and Community

Father, I decree and declare an "already done blessing" over my family, friends, church, and community. You have given me the power to call those things that be not as though they were. I educe my calling power today by faith. I wait patiently for your word to be fulfilled in our lives. I release the host of heavenly angels to work on our behalf. I cancel every wicked device that's formed against your word. I thank you, Father, for the change that will manifest in my family, friends, church, and community.

Heavenly Father, I declare that your blessing and your good things are running us down and taking over us. Everywhere we turn, there is favor. I declare that we are not waiting on the manifestation of your word; by faith we are walking in the manifestation of your word. We receive the rewards of the kingdom now! We declare that things are not getting better; they are already better.

We receive our healing. By the stripes of Jesus, we are healed. I declare we are the healed of the Lord, and we are protecting our health. We walk in forgiveness; therefore, nothing is causing you to withhold our blessing. We will forgive seven times seventy times in a day, if we have to. Wealth and riches are in our homes, our businesses, our churches, and our communities. We are the seed of Abraham, and his blessings are ours.

We speak life over every dead thing. We declare Jehovah Shalom gives us peace. We are whole, with nothing missing and nothing broken. We do not faint in the day of adversity. We will no longer live a defeated life. We will use failure as an opportunity and a step toward bigger and better things. Obstacles will cause us to be more diligent. Our diligent hands shall cause us to rule. We will persist until we succeed. This confession is sealed with the blood of Jesus.

Proverbs 12:24; Ezekiel 37:4; Proverbs 24:10; Judges 6:24

༄ ༅

SPEAK LIFE FOR HEALTH AND LIFESTYLE MANAGEMENT

HEALTH AND HEALING

I confess that my body is the temple of the Holy Spirit; therefore, sickness and disease cannot live in my body. Jesus carried my sins in his own body so that I could live unto righteousness. I declare by the stripes of Jesus, I am healed.

I'm created in the image and likeness of God; therefore, I claim my wholeness. My God brings me health and healing and reveals to me an abundance of prosperity and security.

I speak to my body, and I command it to align with the word of God. I decree health over my flesh. I declare and decree that sickness cannot linger in my body because the Lord, my healer, commands healing in my body.

Even more so, my words are as a honeycomb, sweet to my soul, and health to my bones. Proverbs 12:18 says the tongue of the wise is health. I speak wise words, and I expect health in my body.

I obey and respect my doctor's opinion, but I believe the report of the Lord above everyone else. The prayer of faith will save the sick, and the Lord will raise him up. I confess that I am saved from sickness, and the Lord has raised me up! In the name of Jesus!

Acts 17:28; 1 Corinthians 16:19–20; 1 Peter 2:24; Isaiah 53:4–5; Genesis 1:27; Jeremiah 33:6; Proverbs 16:24; Acts 1; James 5:15

A HEALTHY BODY

I decree and declare that I will honor my body as the temple of the Holy Spirit. Father, your plan is that I prosper and be in health as my soul prospers. I desire to live a long, healthy life. I commit to doing my part by eating nutritious meals, getting rest and exercising daily. I admit that I need your help, and without your help I cannot maintain a healthy lifestyle.

I declare that when I eat and drink, it will not be for taste, but it will be for health, healing, strength, and nutrition. You've made all good things, but all good things are not good for me. Going forth I will make wise food choices. I will not live by bread (natural food only), but I will live by your word. I denounce the spirit of gluttony. I have temperance and control. Your word will be my guide and will help me make better decisions concerning my health.

I declare that according to Exodus 15:26, I will listen carefully to the voice of the Lord, my God, and, Lord, I will do what is right in your eyes. I will pay attention to your commands and keep all your decrees. When I do my part, Lord, you will do your part by not bringing any diseases on me. I declare health and wholeness over my life. Glory!

1 Corinthians 10:31 (ESV); 3 John 1:2; 1 Corinthians 6:12

Peace and Soundness of Mind

I decree and declare God is restoring my mind, my peace, and my joy. As I am being restored, I release every negative, self-defeating thought. I release every hurt, pain, and rejection. I release every negative word that has ever been spoken over my life. I release every stronghold that has been established in my mind, and I let God arise totally over my thoughts.

God is the center of my joy. In God, I have peace and soundness of mind. I live in peace, and I choose to think great thoughts. I constantly think on whatsoever things are true, honest, just, pure, lovely, and of a good report.

I don't worry or have anxiety about anything. I have the peace of God, which passes all understanding. God's peace guards my heart and my mind in Christ Jesus.

2 Thessalonians 3:16 (KJV); Philippians 4:6–8; John 16:33; Isaiah 26:3; 1 Peter 5:7; Matthew 5:9; Romans 15:13; Proverbs 12:12

SPEAK LIFE FOR WEALTH AND PROSPERITY

∞

FAVOR WITH GOD AND MAN

I decree and declare that everywhere I go, I experience the favor of God. Favor causes doors to open for me and requests to be granted before me. Favor causes me to stand confidently before my enemies and to triumph over my persecutors. Favor brings me before kings and men of influence. Favor grants me life and preserves my spirit.

When man says no, favor says yes, not because of who I am, but whose I am. Favor covers me as a shield and causes the angels of the Lord to work on my behalf. I declare God's favor is with me for a lifetime. I will never run out of favor with God and man. No good thing does God withhold from those who walk uprightly. God, help me to walk upright before you all the days of my life.

Luke 2:52; Psalms 5:12; Psalms 30:5; Psalms 41:11

∞

Jesus, You Are My Source

Lord, you are my source. Jesus is the source of my strength, peace, and provision. I will look unto the hills, from which comes my help. My help comes from the Lord.

Sorrows will be with the wicked, but I will trust in the Lord and be surrounded with loving-kindness.

Lord, thank you for running back and forth throughout the whole earth, to show yourself strong on my behalf. I delight in the God of my salvation, knowing that He will give me the desires of my heart in the name of Jesus. You are the greatest source. I praise your Holy Name!

Psalms 37:4; Psalms 27:1; Psalms 32:10

❦

Success, Prosperity, and Wealth

I declare God is positioning my life for success, prosperity, and wealth for his glory. It's His plan that I prosper and be in health as my soul prospers. I receive and embrace God's greatness for my life. I believe that I will receive what God has for my life.

I'm no longer concerned about how I will make things happen in my life. Through obedience, I will allow the word of God to navigate my life toward greatness. I declare that my possibilities are limitless, and I will never run out of options. New doors are opening for me, and new opportunities are coming into my life.

As I succeed, prosper, and increase, I will continue to be a blessing to others.

God is always working behind the scenes on my behalf. He's strategically shifting things in my favor. With God on my side, I will never settle for lack. I decree that all of my needs are met because Jehovah Jireh, my Provider, is forever present in my life.

I decree that the God of promise is more than enough and is able to make all grace, favor, and earthly blessing to come to me in abundance, so that I am always and in all circumstances furnished in abundance for every good work and charitable donation.

I'm not destined to be broke spiritually, emotionally, physically, or economically. God has a predestined inheritance for me. God has prepared the good life for me. I trust and believe that I have received. It's sealed in the Holy Spirit of promise.

3 John 1:2; Isaiah 58:8; Joshua 1:7; 1 Chronicles 22:11; 2 Chronicles 20:20; Psalms 30:5–7; 2 Corinthians 6:16, 18; 2 Corinthians 9:8

ᑯᑋ ᑋᑐ

I DECREE DOUBLES

I decree and declare that this is my year of doubles. The devil has
robbed me in many areas, and now it's payback time. I decree and
declare doubles in everything that was stolen. I declare double
health, double wealth, double favor, double joy, double peace,
double anointing, double increase, double prosperity, double
checks, double discounts, double love, double friendships, double
opportunities, double doors opening, and double blessings. I receive
doubles in Jesus's name!

Exodus 22:4; Exodus 22:7

ᑯᑋ ᑋᑐ

BLESSED

I confess that I am blessed in accordance with Matthew 5:10–16. I am blessed when I do not render evil for evil. I am blessed when evil is done unto me and I rejoice. I am blessed when I love my enemies and those who hate me. I am blessed when I make peace and not war. I am blessed when I show love, mercy, and forgiveness. Therefore, I decree and declare I am blessed with all spiritual blessings in heavenly places in Christ (the anointed one).

As a blessed (woman, man, child of God), I declare that I am the salt of the earth, the light of the world, and I'm like a city that is set on a hill that cannot be hid. I am like a candle on a candlestick, that where ever I go, I give light to all who are around. I will let my light shine before men. When people see my actions, they glorify my heavenly Father. Hallelujah, I'm blessed!

Matthew 5:10–16; Ephesians 1:3

ॐ ~∾

BUSINESS GROWTH

Lord, I ask that you would bless me indeed and enlarge my personal, spiritual, and business territories. I ask that your hand would be with me and that you would keep me from evil. By your spirit, I will operate my businesses in integrity, and I will treat each client fairly and respectfully.

Lord, I thank you for giving me witty ideas and inventions. I thank you for blessing me with the ability to establish, maintain, and grow successful businesses. I thank you, Lord, for empowering me to create employment and opportunities for others. I declare continued success over my businesses. I declare that I am an anointed entrepreneur and businessman/businesswoman. I declare that my businesses will expand to the four corners of the world. I will connect with the right people from all over.

As my businesses continue to grow, I will continue to be a blessing to others. I will continue to give my tithes and offerings. I will distribute portions of all of my increase to help plant, establish, and expand your kingdom throughout the world. I will not become greedy, nor will I overindulge in pleasures.

Father, I thank you in advance for blessing my hands and causing them to prosper. I believe this is my businesses' time and season to prosper. I will experience success on multiple levels and in multiple ways to the praise and glory of God.

Father, I thank you for an increase in wisdom, knowledge, and understanding, which causes me to be a wise businessperson.

1 Chronicles 4:10

∽∾∽∾

FLOURISHING IN FAMINE

I declare I will be satisfied and sustained in times of famine. Not only will I be satisfied, my God will cause me to flourish in the midst of a famine. I will continue to speak the word of God despite the conditions that are before me. I will speak to every mountain and tell it to move. I will continue being faithful to God. I will trust in Jehovah Jireh (my Provider) and El-Shaddai (my All-Sufficient One).

The world may change its system, but I will remain faithful to God's system. God will always show himself strong on behalf of all who seek him and his kingdom first in difficult times. My God will make a way where there seems to be no way. He will bless me abundantly so that I can reach out and be a blessing to the people around me.

Psalms 37:19

∽ ∾

CHEERFUL GIVER

I confess that I am a giver, and, as a giver, more is given to me. I declare that people always give great proportions (good measure— more than enough, pressed down, shaken together, and running over in return) to me.

I give bountifully and in abundance. I know it is more blessed for me to give than to receive. God has blessed me to be a blessing. I am a proactive and intentional giver. I purpose in my heart to give. I give bountifully; therefore, I reap bountifully. I give abundantly, and I reap abundantly.

I do not give grudgingly or out of necessity, but I am a cheerful giver, and God loves a cheerful and prompt giver. My attitude and obedience in giving make it possible for God to make all grace abound toward me so that I have sufficiency of all things that abound to every good work.

I decree that every time I give to the poor, I lend to the Lord. My harvest is always greater than the seed. I am grateful to be able to bless others.

I declare that because I'm a giver, there is no lack in my life. My needs are met, and my bills are paid. My checking and savings accounts are overflowing. My investments are fruitful, and I have plenty more to give. In the name of Jesus! Hallelujah!

Luke 6:38; Acts 20:35; 2 Corinthians 9:6–9; Proverbs 19:17

THE BLESSING OF DEUTERONOMY 28

I decree that the Lord has blessed me with all spiritual blessings in heavenly places in Christ Jesus. I declare the blessings of Deuteronomy 28 over my life.

As I listen carefully to the Lord, my God, to observe and to do all his commandments that he commands me each and every day, my God is setting me on high above all nations of the earth, and all these blessings shall come on me and overtake me.

I declare and decree that as I obey the voice of God, I will be blessed in the city, blessed in the country, and blessed will be the fruit of my body. My children and everything that I produce will be blessed. My substance will continue to increase. I will be blessed when I come in and blessed when I go out.

The Lord will cause the enemies who rise up against me to be defeated before me. They will come out against me one way, but they will flee before me seven ways. The Lord will command the blessing to be upon me and my houses, storehouses, and all that I take on. God will bless me in the place that he gives me. Whatever I set my hands to do will be blessed.

I decree and declare that the Lord will establish me as holy unto himself as I keep His commandments and walk in his ways. Most of all, people will see that I am called by the name of the Lord. The Lord will make me plenteous in goods, and He will open for me His good treasure. I will experience rain and abundance at the right time and right season. I will lend to many nations, and I will not borrow. The Lord will make me the head and not the tail. I will be above only and not beneath as I listen and obey God. I will abide in the word of God. I will not stray to the right hand or to the left to go after other gods to serve them. It is so, and amen!

Deuteronomy 28:1–14

Financial Increase

Father, I ask for wisdom to better manage the finances that come in my home. I'm not relying on my own abilities; I know that it is you who gives me the power to get wealth. As I connect with you in prayer, I ask that you would connect me to the right resources.

As I increase, I will continue to honor your word by giving my tithes and offerings. I will continue to bless others as you bless me. Father, thank you for gracing me with the ability to be a good steward with the resources that are given to me.

As I increase, I will not become greedy or live above my means, but I will prioritize based on my needs. Father, I thank you for your divine intervention to free me from debt. I thank you for breaking every stronghold of lack and releasing unto me abundance.

Now I decree and declare that the things that have hindered me in the past are in the past. I'm coming into what God has for me. Everything that the locust has stolen is being returned.

I speak Isaiah 45:3 over my life. God will give me the treasures of darkness and hidden wealth of secret places, so that I may know and always remember that it is the Lord, the God of Israel, who calls me by my name. I serve the God who is the source of my every need. There is no shortage or lack, and there is more than enough available to meet my needs, spirit, soul, and body. Amen!

∽

SPEAK LIFE TO YOUR PURPOSE

CREATED IN HIS IMAGE AND LIKENESS

I boldly confess that I am uniquely made. I am made in the image and likeness of God. God gave me my own special attributes. I get my identity from God and not from the world. I am a royal priesthood, a holy nation, and a peculiar person. I am beautiful in the eyes of God. The world has its classes for people, but I am in God's class. I'm different, but that's fine because God has called me to be different. I'm not common or average, and I wasn't created to be common or average. I'm God's workmanship, created in Christ Jesus for good works, which God prepared beforehand, that I should walk in. Praise the name of Jesus!

1 Peter 2:9 (KJV); Genesis 1:27 (KJV); Ephesians 2:10 (KJV)

಄ഄ

GOD'S PLAN FOR MY LIFE

I decree and declare that God is showing me his plan for my life. I'm excited that God is bringing his will to pass in my life. My plan is to continuously seek the plan of God. I come against every plot and plan that the enemy has for my life. I cast down wrong thoughts and all opposing forces that come to distract and hinder God's plan for my life. No weapon formed against me shall prosper.

I decree and declare every dream that has birth in the spirit realm shall manifest in the earth. I am not my own; my life belongs to God, and I trust he is masterfully working his plan for my life. The Lord's plans for my life include welfare and not evil. He plans to give me a future and a hope.

Also God has plans to increase me, to open new doors for me, and to take me places beyond what I can ask or think, according to his power that works in me. Therefore, I will accomplish the plans that God has for me. I will trust God to bring the right opportunities across my path and line up the right people to come into my life. God is ordering my steps and stretching me to a new level.

2 Corinthians 10:5; Psalms 37:4; Jeremiah 29:11; Ephesians 3:20; Psalms 77:11–12 (NLT)

The Vision Will Speak

God gave me a vision, and I have written the vision down. I have made it a plan. The vision is for an appointed time. I decree and declare that my time is coming. I will not lose heart, be dismayed, or give up. The vision may not come to pass immediately, but I will continue to work toward it and wait for it.

I will remain hopeful. I have the strength to keep pressing forward. I will complete each assignment that God gives me to bring the vision to pass. I trust God; therefore, I remain in faith. I'm closer today to accomplishing the vision.

The angels of the Lord are working on my behalf. My times are in God's hand. I expect a change at any time. I will receive all that God has for me. My tears will become shouts of joy. I'm coming out with my hands held high in praise. Thank you, Father, for your faithfulness! In the name of Jesus.

Habakkuk 2:2–4

GIFTS AND TALENTS

I activate every gift and talent that God has graced me with. I use my gifts to serve others as a faithful steward who is yielded to God's grace.

I will make the most of my talents and gifts by using them to make a difference in the world. My gifts and talents set me apart from other people.

My gifts and talents bring out the best in me and cause the world to see God through me. God is revealing talents and abilities that I never knew that I had. God takes pleasure in seeing me use what he has given me.

I consider my gifts as an investment from God, and I plan to give God a great return on His investment. I believe that my gifts are constantly making room for me and are bringing me before great men.

1 Peter 4:10

∽∾

Goal Minded

Father, I thank you for not allowing the desires of my heart to go unanswered. I will continue to set and achieve goals in accordance with the purpose for my life. I will continue to thrive and press forward toward my goals. Looking back or turning back is not an option. Giving up is not an option. I may have to reposition myself or change direction, but I will persist until I succeed.

I decree and declare the plan has been written, submitted, and approved. It is in the will. My beginning was small, but I decree and declare my latter days will be very great. I can see the big picture. By faith I can see the end, and it looks much better than it looks right now.

Philippians 3:13, 14 (KJV); Habakkuk 2:2–4; Job 8:7 (ESV)

SPEAK LIFE FOR WISDOM, GUIDANCE, AND PROTECTION

DIVINE PROTECTION

I decree and declare that I am divinely protected. I'm protected from dangers seen and unseen. God protects my going out and coming in. I am guarded against the evil one. The Lord keeps me from all harm, and he watches over my life. God makes even my enemies to be at peace with me.

I reverence and fear God, and he causes his angels to encamp round about me to deliver me from the hand of the enemy. The angel of the Lord fights for me. Therefore, I am more than a conqueror. My battles do not belong to me; they belong to the Lord. I only fight the good fight of faith.

Greater is He (Jesus Christ, the Savior) that is in me than he that is in the world. My Father (God) is faithful, and he will not break his covenant nor alter the thing that is gone out of his lips. His word is settled in heaven! Hallelujah!

Proverbs 16:7; Psalms 121:7; 2 Thessalonians 3:3; Psalms 34:7

Spiritual Warfare

I confess that although I walk in the flesh, I do not war after the flesh. I do not fight against flesh and blood. The weapons of my warfare are not carnal, but mighty through God to the pulling down of strongholds. I aim to destroy and demolish spiritual strongholds. Strongholds in my mind, in my will, and in my bloodline are destroyed.

I decree that I overcome warfare and win battles by casting down imaginations and every high thing that exalts itself against the knowledge of God. I bring into captivity every thought to the obedience of Christ. In the name of Jesus!

2 Corinthians 10:1–6

GOD'S DIRECTION

I decree and declare my steps are ordered in the Lord, and I rely on God to direct my paths. The word of God is a lamp unto my feet and a light unto my path. I am instructed by God, and He teaches me the way that I should go. I am not confused about the paths or directions for my life.

By faith, I believe I'm always directed to the right place at the right time to receive favor, increase, and opportunities. For God know the plans He has for me, plans for welfare and not for evil, to give me a future and a hope.

I declare that I'm focused, and I am allowing God to work in my life. He is leading and guiding me toward the destiny He has for me. In the name of Jesus!

Proverbs 3:5–7; Psalms 119:105; Psalms 37:23

᪥ ᪥

THE VOICE OF GOD

I decree and declare that I listen to what God is saying. God continuously speaks to me. I recognize and listen to my Father's voice. I do not follow the voice of a stranger. My ears are open and sensitive to the voice of God. God helps me to hear what he says.

Psalms 85:8

◦─◦

INCREASE IN WISDOM, KNOWLEDGE, AND UNDERSTANDING

I confess Jesus is made unto me wisdom, righteousness, sanctification, and redemption. I walk in the wisdom of God and not the wisdom of man only. I expect to know what to do in every situation and under all circumstances. I'm never caught with my guard down. I declare that I make wise decisions for my life.

I roll my works upon the Lord, and He makes my thoughts agreeable to His will, and so are my plans established, and they are successful. I understand wisdom that is from God is better than increase and profit from silver and gold.

I do not lack wisdom, because when I need wisdom, I ask God for it, and He gives it to me. I ask in faith and without doubting and without wavering. Therefore, I am not like the surge of the sea, driven by the wind and tossed. I am not double minded or unstable. I am steadfast and unmovable. Wisdom is the principle thing in my life!

Proverbs 3:13–18; James 1:2–11

◦─◦

KINGDOM CITIZENSHIP

Today I present my petitions before the throne of grace, according to the promises of God. Father, your word will not return to you void or without accomplishing your purpose.

I claim my kingdom citizenship. I think, act, and live like a kingdom citizen. My old way of living no longer exists. My new way of living aligns with the word of God.

My belief aligns with your word, which says I am of the kingdom of God and of the kingdom of light. Also your Kingdom is in me. I no longer walk after the flesh, but I walk in the spirit. I walk by faith and not by sight.

As a kingdom citizen, I exercise my right to use my tongue to speak life and not death. I have the power to call those things that be not as though they were. I call forth blessings and not curses. I declare that my tongue is the pen of a ready writer. When I speak, I'm writing my future. I frame my world by the word of God. In the name of Jesus!

Luke 17:20–21

THE BOLDNESS OF CHRIST

Through Christ, I am bold as a lion. I have the courage, strength, and confidence I need to accomplish great things. I am more than a conqueror through Jesus Christ, who loves me and gave his life for me. God is always with me. Therefore, I declare if God is for me, who can stand against me? With the Lord as my helper, I will not fear what man tries to do to me. Daily I wait on the Lord, and He strengthens my heart.

David was anointed to face and conquer Goliath, and I am anointed to conquer every giant in my life. I don't have conversations with doubt talkers. All persecutors, naysayers, critics, and accusers are being slayed in the spirit, and their words cannot stop me. I choose to listen to what God is saying. Thank you, God, for calling, choosing, and equipping me to walk boldly in the earth.

Romans 8:37; Proverbs 28:1; Hebrews 13:6; Joshua 1:9;
Psalms 27:14

SPEAK LIFE BY FAITH

FAITH, HOPE, AND EXPECTATION

I confess that I walk in expectation. My expectations shall be fulfilled. I see great things happening for me and good things coming in my life.

I expect the impossible to happen in my life. I decree that nothing shall be impossible for me, because I'm a believer and not a doubter. I'm prompted and directed by the Holy Spirit to expect great things. The Holy Spirit is my comforter. He leads and guides me into all truth.

In the midst of opposition and disappointments, I expect great results. My expectation is contingent on the fulfilment of the promises of God, who is faith that promises. I decree and declare that I will live the life that Jesus came to give me: a life that is filled with abundance even more than what I currently possess. There is no room for doubt, lack, and decrease.

Today I declare that now my faith is the substance of things I hope for and the evidence of things I can't see. I patiently wait on what I hope for. My hope cancels out doubt. Through faith, I have access to grace, and I stand in God's grace.

Thank you, Lord, for giving me faith, hope, and expectation!

Romans 8:24; Psalms 147:11; Proverbs 13:12; John 10:10; Jeremiah 33:6; Hebrews 11:1

❧

FAITH AND WORKS

I decree and declare that I am a doer of the word, and not a hearer only. I will not deceive myself by being a hearer only. I am a blessed doer of the word.

The Bible declares, "Faith without works is dead." I decree and declare that I have faith with works. I put the word to work in my life. I put faith to work in my life. Faith is being made perfect in me. I believe what Jesus said, and, according to my faith, it will be done unto me. In Jesus's name, I decree it to be!

James 2:14–24

FAITH AND PATIENCE

Father, I believe your promises are "yes and amen." You sent Jesus Christ to die so that I can live and have life more abundantly. You have given me the measure of faith to ensure that I have everything I need to walk by faith and not by sight.

Today I declare that as a child of God, I will no longer allow my flesh or my eyes to dictate the outcome of my situation. Through faith and patience, I will inherit the promises of God, so I decree and declare that the promises of God are manifesting in my life.

Going forward, I will have patience and faith in the midst of persecutions and tribulations. I will follow those (the giants of faith) who, through faith and patience, inherit the promises of God.
I believe that I receive according to my faith. In the name of Jesus!

Hebrews 6:12; Hebrews 10:38; Galatians 3:11; Romans 1:17

SPEAK LIFE FOR ENCOURAGEMENT AND MENTAL WELLNESS

THE JOY OF THE LORD IS MY STRENGTH

I decree and declare that I will not be robbed of the joy that has been given me through the blood of Jesus. I will use my joy to influence and inspire others. I'm not going to live another day sad, negative, discouraged, and unfulfilled. I decree and declare that the joy of the Lord Is my strength.

I decree and declare that the oil of gladness the Lord has assigned to my head will not run dry. I'm anointed for joy and strength. This joy I have, the world didn't give it to me, and the world can't take it away.

Shouts of victory and celebrations of joy shall be heard daily throughout my household. Hallelujah!

1 Peter 1:8 (NIV); Nehemiah 8:10 (NIV); 2 Timothy 2:22 (NIV); Psalms 45:7

≈

JOY, JOY, GOD'S GREAT JOY

Today I confess that I have God's great joy down in my soul. I have joy down in my soul. I have sweet, beautiful, soul-saving joy in my soul. My joy is complete in Christ Jesus.

My joy isn't based on what I have or don't have. Neither is it based on what someone does or doesn't do for me. My joy is based totally on my trust in God. I declare, the joy of the Lord is my strength.

According to the word of God, anger, sadness, frustrations, and agitations are with me only for a moment, but joy comes every morning. My joy is refreshed each morning along. Every morning I receive a fresh dose of joy and the new mercies of God. Daily I will shout for joy and declare God's goodness, because I know my Father is working in my defense. My joy, peace, and soundness of mind have been sealed in heaven. I have fullness of joy, and at my right hand are pleasures forever more. There is nothing and no one who can steal my joy.

I declare that the joy of my salvation is restored and I'm upheld by the power of God's spirit.

Psalms 5:11; Psalms 51:12; Psalms 42:4

≈

TODAY

Today I confess that the mercies of God are new to me. Today is a new day. I declare it to be a great and wonderful day. Today I'm living a more than conqueror's life. Today I speak peace, love, and joy over my life. Today I frame my world by the word of God. I rejoice today in God's goodness and his glory. Today I declare my circumstances are changing for the better. Today I determine to be happy despite any challenges.

Today is the day the Lord has made, and I will rejoice and be glad in it. Today is a great day to praise God and give Him thanks. In the name of Jesus.

Psalms 118:24 (NIV); Hebrews 11:3

∽

STARTING OVER

I believe; therefore, I will confess. In the name of Jesus, I let go of my past and declare that it's behind me. My past can't harm or hurt me. It can only help push me toward a brighter future.

I declare that I am a new creation in Christ. I am walking in the newness of life. I press forth, forward, past the pain, hurts, challenges, and tests, and this is how I do it: I press forward by forgetting those things that are behind and reaching forth toward what's before me. I press toward the mark for the prize of the high calling of God that is in Christ Jesus.

As I start over, I decree, according to Isaiah 43:19, Behold (listen carefully), God is doing a new thing in my life, and now it will spring forth. People won't even understand it, but He shall make a way in the wilderness and rivers in the desert. Now is the moment and the appointed time. I have patiently waited for the Lord. He has renewed my strength and caused me to mount up on wings as eagles, to run and not get weary, and to walk and not faint.

Thank you, Lord, for this new season of my life. Thank you for this season of increase and favor. I've been changed. I praise you for a new heart and a new spirit. I no longer have a heart of stone, but a heart of flesh. I thank you for a great start!

Philippians 3:13–21 (KJV); Ephesians 4:22–24; Isaiah 43:19; 2 Corinthians 5:17 (KJV); Isaiah 40:31

∽∘∾

SPEAK LIFE WHEN YOU'RE STANDING IN THE GAP

~~ ❧ ~~

OUR SPIRITUAL LEADERS

Father, today I lift up all pastors and church leaders. I declare that our leaders are honorable and faithful men and women of God who love God with all of their heart, soul, mind and strength. Our men and women of God are committed to cultivating godly character and integrity in their congregation. I declare they are transparent and genuine. Whatever they do in the dark, they can do in the light. Whatever they set their hands to do, they do it heartily unto the Lord. They are not men pleasers.

I confess the spirit of God operates through the heart of our leaders by His power. Our leaders are diligent in their pursuit to follow biblical principles. God has granted unto our pastors and leaders all things that pertain to life and godliness, through the knowledge of him who called them to his own glory and excellence.

I decree and declare that our leaders are wise stewards of their finances. Therefore, God will supply their every need, according to his riches in glory in Christ Jesus.

Our leaders will not cause the congregation to perish due to their lack of vision. They have a clear written vision for the congregation.

The vision is effectively communicated. They genuinely desire to keep the congregation united and in harmony one with another.

Our leaders are always tapping into new levels in the spirit realm. Signs and wonders do follow them. I decree a flesh anointing on their ministry and an increased anointing for miracles. In Jesus's name!

Philippians 4:19 (KJV); 1 Timothy 1:5 (KJV); 2 Peter 1:3 (ESV); Ephesians 3:23–24; Proverbs 29:18

～

GOD BLESS AMERICA

Lord, I pray that you will bless America even as you have many
times before.

The earth is yours and the fullness of it, the world and they that
dwell therein. You are Lord of the nations.

Lord, every president and government official's heart is in your
hand, and you turn it however you will. I pray that you will direct
the hand of our political leaders. I pray that you will raise leaders in
America who are honest and trustworthy and have integrity and
morality. I pray you would extend wisdom, strength, and prudence
to our present and future president and government officials. I pray
that our leaders will rely on your strength and not their own power
when it comes to making the right decision.

I ask that you would grant America favor with other countries. I
pray that America will continue to be a country that operates in
freedom and not bondage. I praise you for the freedom to serve you
openly. I pray for unity and peace in America and across the world.

Lord, you said, "If my people, who are called by my name, shall
humble themselves and pray and seek my face and turn from their

131

wicked ways, then will I hear from heaven and will forgive their sin and will heal their land." I pray that America will meet every condition in order to receive forgiveness and healing in our land. In the name of Jesus!

Psalms 24:1; Proverbs 21:1; 2 Chronicles 7:14

Keep the Word of the Lord on Your Heart!

Psalms 119:11 (ESV)
I have stored up your word in my heart, that I might not sin against you.

Matthew 12:36 (NIV)
But I tell you that everyone will have to give account on the day of judgment for every empty word they have spoken.

Hebrews 11:3 (NIV)
Through faith we understand that the worlds were framed by the word of God, so that things which are seen were not made of things which do appear.

Matthew 12:37 (NIV)
For by your words you will be justified, and by your words you will be condemned.

Proverbs 16:24
Pleasant words are as a honeycomb, sweet to the soul, and health to the bones.

Psalms 45:1
My heart is indicting a good matter: I speak of the things which I have made touching the king: my tongue is the pen of a ready writer.

Psalms 81:10 (NIV)
Open wide your mouth, and I will fill it.

❧ ❧

Speak I Am

Look yourself in the mirror and declare what God says about you.

1. I am a new creature in Christ. *2 Corinthians 5:17*
2. I am redeemed from the curse of sin, sickness, and poverty. *Deuteronomy 28; Galatians 3:13*
3. I am fearfully and wonderfully made; your works are wonderful, I know that full well. *Psalms 139:14*
4. I am a child of God. *John 1:12*
5. I am a friend of Jesus. *John 15:15*
6. I am no longer a slave to sin. *Romans 6:6*
7. I am crucified with Christ. *Romans 6:6*
8. I am free from the law of sin and death. *Romans 8:1*
9. I am a child of God. *Romans 8:17*
10. I am a fellow heir with Christ. *Romans 8:17*
11. I am joined to the Lord and am one spirit with Him. *1 Corinthians 6:17*
12. I am one with all who are in Christ Jesus. *Galatians 3:28*
13. I am a son/daughter and heir of Jesus Christ. *Galatians 4:7*
14. I am chosen, holy, and blameless before God. *Ephesians 1:4*

15. I am redeemed and forgiven by the riches of Christ's grace. *Ephesians 1:7*

16. I am sealed with the Holy Spirit of promise. *Ephesians 1:13*

17. I am seated in the heavenly places with Christ. *Ephesians 2:6*

18. I am God's workmanship, created in Christ Jesus for good works prepared by God. *Ephesians 2:10*

19. I am a member of Christ's body and a partaker of His promise. *Ephesians 3:6; Ephesians 5:30*

20. I am no longer in darkness, but now I am light in the Lord. *Ephesians 5:8; 1 Peter 2:9*

21. I am a citizen of heaven. *Philippians 3:20*

22. I am chosen of God, and I am holy and beloved. *Colossians 3:12; 1 Thessalonians 1:4*

23. I am able to do all things through Christ, who strengthens me. *Philippians 4:13*

24. I am a believer, and the light of the Gospel shines in my mind. *2 Corinthians 4:4*

25. I am a doer of the Word and blessed in my actions. *James 1:22, 25*

26. I am part of a chosen generation, a royal priesthood, a holy nation, a purchased people. *1 Peter 2:9*

27. I am healed by the stripes of Jesus. *Isaiah 53:5; 1 Peter 2:24*

28. I am the salt of the earth. I am the light of the world. A city that is set on a hill cannot be hid. *Matthew 5:13, 14*

29. I am more than a conqueror through Jesus Christ that loves me. *Romans 8:37*

30. I am strengthened with all might, according to His glorious power. *Colossians 1:11*

Thirty Promises of God

There are over two thousand promises in the Bible. I've included thirty promises to remind you of the great, awesome, and faithful God that we serve.

1. And, behold, this day I am going the way of all the earth: and ye know in all your hearts and in all your souls, that not one thing hath failed of all the good things which the LORD your God spake concerning you; all are come to pass unto you, and not one thing hath failed thereof. *Joshua 23:14 (KJV)*

2. For his anger lasts only a moment, but his favor lasts a lifetime; weeping may stay for the night, but rejoicing comes in the morning. *Psalms 30:5 (NIV)*

3. You will experience all these blessings *if* you obey the Lord your God: You will be blessed in your towns and in the country. You will be blessed with many children and productive fields. You will be blessed with fertile herds and flocks. You will be blessed with baskets overflowing with fruit, and with kneading bowls filled with bread. You will be blessed

wherever you go, both in coming and in going. The Lord will conquer your enemies when they attack you...And the Lord will bless everything you do and will fill your storehouses with grain. *Deuteronomy 28:2–8 (NLT)*

4. Blessed is the one who does not walk in step with the wicked or stand in the way that sinners take or sit in the company of mockers, but whose delight is in the law of the Lord, and who meditates on his law day and night. That person is like a tree planted by streams of water, which yields its fruit in season and whose leaf does not wither—whatever they do prospers. *Psalms 1:1–3 (NIV)*

5. "Bring the whole tithe into the storehouse, that there may be food in my house. Test me in this," says the Lord Almighty, "and see if I will not throw open the floodgates of heaven and pour out so much blessing that you will not have room enough for it." Malachi 3:10 (NIV)

6. I will cause my people and their homes around my holy hill to be a blessing. And I will send showers, showers of blessings, which will come just when they are needed." *Ezekiel 34:26 (NLT)*

7. Blessed is the man who listens to me, watching daily at my doors, waiting at my doorway. *Proverbs 8:34 (KJV)*

8. Blessed is he who considers the poor; The Lord will deliver him in time of trouble. The Lord will preserve him and keep him alive, And he will be blessed on the earth; You will not deliver him to the will of his enemies. *Psalms 41:1–2 (NIV)*

9. Nay, in all these things we are more than conquerors through him that loved us. *Romans 8:37*

10. The LORD watches over the foreigner and sustains the fatherless and the widow, but he frustrates the ways of the wicked. *Psalms 146:9 (NIV)*

11. For the LORD God is a sun and shield; the LORD bestows favor and honor; no good thing does he withhold from those whose walk is blameless. *Psalms 84:11 (NIV)*

12. No temptation has overtaken you except what is common to mankind. And God is faithful; he will not let you be tempted beyond what you can bear. But when you are tempted, he will also provide a way out so that you can endure it. *1 Corinthians 10:13*

13. You will seek me and find me when you seek me with all your heart. *Jeremiah 29:13 (NIV)*

14. The LORD bless you and keep you. *Numbers 6:24*

15. But he said to me, "My grace is sufficient for you, for my power is made perfect in weakness." Therefore I will boast all the more gladly about my weaknesses, so that Christ's power may rest on me. *2 Corinthians 12:9 (NIV)*

16. The promise is for you and your children and for all who are far off—for all whom the Lord our God will call. *Acts 2:39 (NIV)*

17. And without faith it is impossible to please God, because anyone who comes to him must believe that he exists and that he rewards those who earnestly seek him. *Hebrews 11:6 (NIV)*

18. This is the confidence we have in approaching God: that if we ask anything according to his will, he hears us. *1 John 5:14*

19. Those who know your name trust in you, for you, LORD, have never forsaken those who seek you. *Psalms 9:10 (NIV)*

20. Now the Lord is the Spirit, and where the Spirit of the Lord is, there is freedom. *2 Corinthians 3:17 (NIV)*

21. He heals the brokenhearted and binds up their wounds. *Psalms 147:3*

22. He will call on me, and I will answer him; I will be with him in trouble, I will deliver him and honor him. With long life I will satisfy him and show him my salvation." *Psalms 91:15–16*

23. I will instruct you and teach you in the way you should go; I will counsel you with my loving eye on you. *Psalms 32:8*

24. I make known the end from the beginning, from ancient times, what is still to come. I say, " My purpose will stand, and I will do all that I please." *Isaiah 46:9–10 (NIV)*

25. For the eyes of the Lord are on the righteous and his ears are attentive to their prayer, but the face of the Lord is against those who do evil. *1 Peter 3:12 (NIV)*

26. The LORD gives strength to his people; the LORD blesses his people with peace. *Psalms 29:11*

27. And God is able to bless you abundantly, so that in all things at all times, having all that you need, you will abound in every good work. *2 Corinthians 9:8 (NIV)*

28. The angel of the LORD encamps around those who fear him, and he delivers them. *Psalms 34:7*

29. He will cover you with his feathers, and under his wings you will find refuge; his faithfulness will be your shield and rampart. *Psalms 91:4 (NIV)*

30. The LORD will fight for you; you need only to be still. *Exodus 14:14 (NIV)*

The Word Exchange

Let's exchange lifeless words for life-giving words.

You are so stupid. You are so ignorant. You are so dumb.

- *You are smart. The wisdom of God is arising in your life.*
  You will begin to make good decisions. I declare that you
  are smart. You are able to comprehend well.

I hate you.

- *I love you with the love of God.*

You act just like your (father, mother, etc.).

- *God has made you in His image and after His likeness.*
  You have the behaviors and character of your heavenly
  Father.

You make me sick.

- *I praise God for my spouse to be. He/she fears God. He/she walks in favor. God is preparing me for my spouse and my spouse for me. When we meet, we both shall be whole people. I have the strength to deal with whatever or whoever is in my presence.*

I wish I were dead.

- *I thank God for the gift of life. Things are getting better.*

I wish you would die.

- *I thank God for you being a part of my life.*

You are fat. You are skinny.

- *You are beautifully and wonderfully made.*

I wish I had not married you.

- *I declare that you are the apple of my eye. I thank God for how He continues to work on both of us.*

I wish I had not given birth to you.

- *You are a perfect gift to me from God.*

You will never be anything. You are a loser. You were born to fail.

⊣ *You were born to succeed. No weapon formed against you shall prosper.*

I'm always broke. I don't have any money.

⊣ *God's plan for me is to prosper me and give me a great future. I will plant bountifully, and I will reap bountifully.*

I can't do that. It's too hard.

⊣ *I can do all things through Christ, who strengthens me.*

The doctors said I'm dying.

⊣ *I shall live and not die and shall declare the works of the Lord. I will not die when man says I will, but I will die when God says so. I call healing into my life.*

Quick Reference Faith Statements

This collection of faith statements is meant to be used as a quick point of reference when there is a need to speak God's word quickly to avoid speaking against your particular concern. These faith statement are in no way intended to replace your Bible study and meditation time. They reference only a few facets of your life.

Before they call I will answer; while they are still speaking I will hear.
Isaiah 65:24

Abundance
Jesus, thank you for giving me life and giving it to me in abundance. By faith I decree that my life overflows with abundance. *John 10:10*

Anger
Lord, I thank you for being gracious and full of compassion, slow to anger, and of great mercy. I believe that I am gracious, compassionate, slow to anger, and merciful. *Psalms 145:5*

Belief

I confess according to *Mark 9:23*; I can believe and I do believe all things are possible. There is nothing too hard for God.

Children

Great is the Lord's peace upon my children. They have been taught of the Lord. My children are the glory of their Father. *Proverbs 17:6; Isaiah 54:13*

Encouragement

I shall not be moved by my trials and tribulations. I have cast every burden upon the Lord, and He is sustaining me. *Psalms 55:22*

Faith

Today I walk by faith and not by sight. My faith is the substance of things that I hope for and the evidence of things I cannot see. *2 Corinthians 5:7; Hebrews 11:1*

Fear

I agree with God's word. God has not given me a spirit of fear, but a spirit of power, and of love, and of a sound mind. *2 Timothy 1:7*

Forgiveness

Heavenly Father, when people do me wrong, I find it in my heart to forgive them, and when I do wrong, you forgive my trespasses. Thank you for giving me a forgiving heart. *Matthew 6:14*

Guidance

My steps are ordered in the Lord, and I delight in His ways. In all my ways, I acknowledge the Lord, and He directs my paths. *Psalms 37:23; Proverbs 3:6*

Healing

I will bless the Lord, O my soul, and I will not forget all his benefits. He forgives all my iniquity, heals all my diseases, redeems my life from the pit, and crowns me with steadfast love and mercy. *Psalms 103:2–4*

Honesty

The more truth I know, the freer I become. The more I walk in integrity, the more favor I have with God. *John 8:32; 2 Corinthians 8:21*

Hope

I do not put all of my hope in man, but I hope in the Lord. I rejoice in hope because I know the plans the Lord has for me. Plans for welfare and not for evil, to give me a future and a hope. *Jeremiah 29:11; Romans 12:12*

Joy

The joy of the Lord is my strength. My joyful heart is good like medicine. I declare that I rejoice in hope, I remain patient in tribulation, and I'm constantly in prayer. I count it all joy when I'm faced with various kinds of trials. *Romans 12:12; James 1:2*

Laziness

I refuse to settle for laziness, mediocrity, and a slack hand. Everything I set my hands to do works in my favor, because the hand of the diligent makes rich. The soul of the lazy will crave and will receive nothing, but the soul of the diligent is richly supplied. *Proverbs 13:4; Proverbs 10:4*

Marriage

My marriage honors God and gives Him glory. My spouse and I speak kind words to each other. We are patient and kind to each other. We do not envy or resent each other. Our goal is to be a light to other couples and to please God by demonstrating His love and support. *Hebrews 13:4*

Mercy

I show mercy to others, and I'm grateful that God shows me mercy. Blessed are the merciful, for they shall receive mercy. *Matthew 5:7*

Money

I have chosen to serve God and not money. I use money as an opportunity to bless the kingdom of God, to bless others, and to better my life. Money is not my source; God is my source. *Matthew 6:24*

Patience

In patience I possess my soul. I will receive the promises of God through my faith and patience. *Hebrews 6:15; Hebrews 10:36*

Peace

Thank you, Lord, for giving me peace that passes all understanding and keeping me in perfect peace as I keep my mind on you. *Isaiah 26:3*

Poverty

I call my life blessed. I declare that I'm prospering and in health as my soul prospers. I'm not destined to live in poverty. I will give my way out of poverty. Greater is coming to me. *3 John 1:2*

Power

"God is able to do far more abundantly than all that I ask or think, according to the power at work within me." *Ephesians 3:20*

Prayer

I'm not anxious about anything, but in everything by prayer and supplication with thanksgiving I make known my request to God. As I ask in prayer, it is given to me. As I seek, I will find, and when I know, it will be open to me. *Philippians 4:6; Luke 11:9*

Success

I will continue to be strong and courageous while I carefully observe and do all that the Lord my God commands me to do. I will keep the word of God close to my heart. I will meditate on the word day and night and do according to what is written in the word. For then I will make my way prosperous, and I will have good success. *Joshua 1:9*

Trust

In God I will trust, and I will not be afraid. I trust in the Lord with all of my heart. Since God is for me, who can be against me? *Psalms 56:3–4; Romans 8:31; Proverbs 3:5–7*

Wisdom

I decree and declare that I seek wisdom from above which is first pure, then peaceable, gently, open to reason, full of mercy and good fruits, impartial and sincere. *James 3:17*

Work

When I work, I work heartily as for the Lord and not for men. I commit my work to the Lord, and my plans are established. I know that I will receive an inheritance as a reward.

Proverbs 16:3

THE SPEAK LIFE CHALLENGE

Proverbs 12:18 (ESV)
There is one whose rash words are like sword thrusts, but the
tongue of the wise brings healing.

Proverbs 18:21 (KJV)
Death and life are in the power of the tongue: and they that love
it shall eat the fruit thereof.

WE ALL HAVE said words that we wish we could recant. Maybe you are the parent who has called your child "dummy," "idiot," "stupid," or "ugly" or the spouse who has called your mate "fat," "no good," or "sorry" or the coach who has called your team "worthless" or "losers"; nevertheless, words can cause a lot of emotional pain.

The more we hear, read, or speak a word or phrase, the more power it has over us. Romans 10:17 reads, "so faith comes from hearing, and hearing through the word of Christ." Well, doubt comes by hearing through negative words. If we want our faith to increase and our lives to improve, we must develop more confidence by consistently hearing faith-filled words. On the other hand, our confidence and self-esteem begins to diminish when we consistently hear negative words. A person will gravitate to and believe in what he/she hears most.

Think about how hard it is to forget the things you've heard over and over, such as the ABCs, multiplication tables, your social security number, and nursery rhythms. Most of them you will never forget. It's the same way with words, whether good or bad.

My life is God's gift to me, and how I live it and what I do with it is my gift to God. God has charged me to imitate him by speaking life and challenging others to speak life. My mission is to start a speak life epidemic. I plan to accomplish this by engaging my readers, family members, church members, and friends to speak life one word, one sentence and one paragraph at a time. I charge you to join the Speak Life Challenge. You will become an architect of your life, and you will help others to do the same.

I challenge you to:

1. Avoid name-calling at any time.
2. Deliberately say something nice to someone that you don't know.
3. Deliberately say something nice to someone who you know casually and personally.

4. Each time you hear someone say something negative about another person, you respond by saying something nice about the same person.
5. Each day, let your first words be to God and your next words be to yourself. Speak life (faith, healing, joy, etc.) to yourself immediately after you speak to God.
6. Go on a fast from (go without) speaking negative words for one day, then two days, then three days, and continue to increase the number of days until you have no remembrance of the last time you've spoken a negative word.
7. Invite someone else to take the Speak Life Challenge with you.
8. Write and post one life-giving statement each day for seven consecutive days.
9. The last thing I will ask of you is to make sure you go to www.facebook.com/cynthialifeuniversity/ and www.cynthialifeu.com to join the Speak Life Challenge Campaign.

Who are you?

What is your vision?

_____
_____
_____
_____
_____
_____
_____
_____
_____
_____
_____
_____
_____
_____
_____
_____
_____
_____
_____
_____
_____
_____
_____
_____
_____
_____
_____
_____

What are you expecting to happen great today?

_____

_____

_____

_____

_____

_____

_____

_____

_____

_____

_____

_____

_____

_____

_____

_____

_____

_____

_____

_____

_____

_____

_____

_____

_____

_____

_____

For more information and to contact
Cynthia A. Golson-Steele:

Info@cynthialifeu.com
Speaklife1@outlook.com
www.cynthialifeu.com

Cynthia Life University
c/o Cynthia A. Golson-Steele
PO Box 2422
Evans, GA 30809

www.facebook.com/cynthialifeuniversity/
Instagram: @cynthialifeu
LinkedIn: Cynthia A Golson Steele
Twitter: @cynthiaslifeu

Hashtags: #speaklife, #cynthialifeuniversity, #cynthialifeu, #speak-
lifechallenge, #speakiwin, #speakiam

Prayer of Salvation

Heavenly Father, I come to you in the name of Your Son, Jesus Christ. You said in your word that whosoever shall call upon the name of the Lord shall be saved (Romans 10:13). Father, I am calling on Jesus right now. I believe He died on the cross for my sins, that He was raised from the dead on the third day, and that He's alive right now.

Lord Jesus, I am asking you now, come into my heart. Live your life in me and through me. I repent of my sins and surrender myself totally and completely to you. Heavenly Father, by faith I now confess Jesus Christ as my new Lord, and from this day forward, I dedicate my life to serving Him.

Your name _____

Today's date _____

About the Author

Cynthia Alana Golson-Steele was raised and educated in Philadelphia, Pennsylvania. She currently resides in Evans, Georgia. Loving and embracing life under grace, Cynthia is the owner of Cynthia Life University Coaching and Training Center and founder of the Speak Life Challenge Campaign.

She is a minister, certified life coach, inspirational speaker, entrepreneur, professional customer service trainer, and Christian leadership trainer. Cynthia is a very active member of Crown Christian Church International, currently serving as senior administrative minister. Cynthia is an active member and supporter of several local organizations. She was a previous member of Toastmasters International and Cambridge Who's Who among Executive and Professional Women.

As a minister, Cynthia unapologetically and unashamedly uses her voice and life experiences as a platform to introduce others to Christ. As a life coach, she works diligently with her clients to make their life POP by challenging them to maximize their purpose, opportunities, and potential (POP).

Her transparency and commitment to help maximize greatness in others has earned her respect and creditability as a trusted voice among her peers, family, friends, and church. Cynthia is serving her kingdom purpose by being a midwife to help others give birth to their purpose.

Cynthia loves spending time with her family, traveling, and inspiring others.

She believes she was created to inspire people to maximize the greatness within!